Golden Ecco Ant

1. Mark Strand, *The Golde...*
2. Carolyn Kizer, *100 Great Poems by women*
3. Jorie Graham, *Earth Took of Earth*

Books by Carolyn Kizer

Poetry

Harping On: Poems 1985–1995
The Ungrateful Garden
Knock Upon Silence
Midnight Was My Cry
YIN: New Poems
Mermaids in the Basement
The Nearness of You

Prose

Proses: On Poems and Poets
Picking and Choosing: Prose on Prose

Translations

Carrying Over
The Splintered Mirror (with Donald Finkel)

Anthologies

The Essential Clare
Leaving Taos
Woman Poet: The West

100
GREAT POEMS
BY WOMEN

A Golden Ecco
Anthology

❑

Edited by
CAROLYN KIZER

THE ECCO PRESS

Please note: The Estate of Elizabeth Bishop would not grant permission to include
Bishop's poem in this anthology.

THE ECCO PRESS
100 West Broad Street
Hopewell, New Jersey 08525
Published simultaneously in Canada by
Penguin Books Canada Ltd., Ontario
Printed in the United States of America
Designed by Debby Jay

FIRST PAPERBACK EDITION

Library of Congress Cataloging-in-Publication Data

One hundred great poems by women : a golden Ecco anthology / edited
by Carolyn Kizer
p. cm.
ISBN 0-88001-422-9
0-88001-581-0 (paperback)
1. American poetry – Women authors. 2. English poetry – Women
authors. 3. Women – Poetry. I. Kizer, Carolyn.
PS589.048 1995
811.008'09287 – dc20 95-9762

The text of this book is set in Cochin
Pages 177 through 184 constitute a continuation of this page.

9 8 7 6 5 4 3 2 1

CONTENTS

PREFACE

———

A collection of poems by women that covers more than five hundred years poses particular difficulties. In assembling these poems I discovered to my dismay that my favorite anthologists, from de la Mare and Auden down to the present, include *no* women poets—or at most one or two—until the middle of the nineteenth century, when Mrs. Browning (not as regularly as Robert) and the Brontës might diffidently step forward. Initial outrage leads to sustained research, which produces twenty excellent women writing between the midfifteenth century and the midnineteenth: five women per century. So the eminent anthologists, though all male, naturally, can't simply be branded male chauvinists. But where, then, were the women? Of our twenty (not including Anonymous), most were titled: countesses, a baroness, duchesses, ladies. Reflect that married women until recently were pregnant most of their adult lives until menopause—if they should live so long. Ten to twenty children was the norm (with a horrifying number of stillbirths and infant deaths). These titled dames could command a host of servants to raise their children and provide them with a little leisure in which to write. Only poor Mary Leapor, spinster, dead at twenty-four, came from the working class. Later, when the aristocratic ladies gave up literature—or gave up circulating it;—it is the spinsters who predominate, from the Brontës right down to Marianne Moore.

Reflect further on the correspondence between those two stars, Virginia Woolf and her sister Vanessa, in which the predominant theme is their anxiety about finding some poor tweeny to empty the slops. Plumbing and birth control and the vote have been instrumental in allowing women to write.

A collection such as this naturally reflects the passions and prejudices of the anthologist, but most of all it draws on the repository of memory: of names, of phrases, of stanzas stored over a lifetime. Sarah Cleghorn's quatrain or "The Battle-Hymn of the Republic" are remembered word for word. But more often it is an evanescence, as transient as joy or sorrow, a whiff of irony, a flick of wit, that sends one back to the source for verification.

"Quote me a memorable line!" Theodore Roethke used to growl to his students. This collection is full of memorable lines, not the least those included in "Delilah," by Ella Wheeler Wilcox, a poem so exquisitely awful that it never can be quite erased from the mind.

I regret that for reasons of space some long poems so seamless that they cannot be excerpted have had to be omitted: Book I of "Aurora Leigh," Miss Rossetti's "Goblin Market," and the contemporary "The City of God," by Robin Morgan, all remarkable works that no reader should overlook.

But to return to passion and prejudice: I am passionately opposed to the notion, held for so long, that womens' true subjects are "love and loss" (having been tagged with that myself). Too often women have collaborated in this male view. But women intensely involved in social concerns have been slotted into the old "love and loss" category: Mrs. Browning, who wrote about child labor, slavery, Italian freedom, and women's rights, is remembered for counting the ways she loved Mr. Browning. Edna Millay, in addition to burning her candle at both ends, burned with indignation about the judicial murder of Sacco and Vanzetti and also wrote memorably about women's rights. I have tried to redress the balance in these cases and in general have favored poems which are "gender neutral." There is very little included here about motherhood and children (only one baby, and the poem is from the baby's point of view). This anthology is bent on showing what women can write about besides romance and domesticity. This, unfortunately, has led to the omission of many fine and sensitive poets who largely confine themselves to the traditional subjects. Many of them are my friends, and I hope that they will forgive me.

CAROLYN KIZER

100 GREAT POEMS
BY WOMEN

ANONYMOUS

(15th century, British)

———

from *The Flower and the Leaf*

And as I sat, the briddes herkning thus,
Me thought that I herd voices sodainly,
The most sweetest and most delicious
That ever any wight, I trow trewly,
Herde in his lyf, for (that) the armony
And sweet accord was in so good musyk,
That the voice to angels most was lyk.

At the last, out of a grove even by,
That was right goodly and plesaunt to sight,
I sy where there cam singing lustily
A world of ladies; but to tell aright
Their greet beautè, it lyth not in my might,
Ne their array; nevertheless, I shal
Tell you a part, though I speke not of al.

In surcotes whyte, of veluet wel sitting,
They were (y)clad; and the semes echoon,
As it were a maner garnishing,
Was set with emeraudes, oon and oon,
By and by; but many a riche stoon
Was set (up-)on the purfils, out of dout,
Of colours, sleves, and traines round about;

As gret(e) perles, round and orient,
Diamondes fyne and rubies rede,
And many another stoon, of which I want
The names now; and everich on her hede,
A riche fret of gold, which, without drede,
Was ful of statly riche stones set;
And every lady had a chapelet

On her hede, of (leves) fresh and grene,
So wel (y-)wrought, and so mérveilously,
That it was a noble sight to sene;
Some of laurer, and some ful plesauntly
Had chapelets of woodbine, and sadly
Some of *agnus-castus* ware also
Chapelets fresh; but there were many tho

That daunced and eek song ful soberly;
But all they yede in maner of compas.
But oon ther yede in-mid the company
Sole by her-self; but al folowed the pace
(Which) that she kept, whos hevenly-figured face
So plesaunt was, and her wel-shape persòn,
That of beautè she past hem everichon.

And more richly beseen, by manifold,
She was also, in every maner thing;
On her hede, ful plesaunt to behold,
A crowne of gold, rich for any king;
A braunch of *agnus-castus* eek bering
In her hand; and, to my sight, trewly,
She lady was of (al) the company.

And she began a roundel lustily,
That *Sus le foyl de vert moy* men call,
Seen, et mon joly cuer endormi;
And than the company answéred all
With voice(s) swete entuned and so small,
That me thought it the sweetest melody
That ever I herde in my lyf, soothly.

And thus they came(n), dauncing and singing,
Into the middes of the mede echone,
Before the herber, where I was sitting,
And, god wot, me thought I was wel bigon;
For that I might avyse hem, on and on,
Who fairest was, who coud best dance or sing,
Or who most womanly was in al thing.

ELIZABETH OF YORK

(1465–1503, British)

———

I Pray to Venus

My heart is set upon a lusty pin;
I pray to Venus of good continuance,
For I rejoice the case that I am in,
Deliver'd from sorrow, annex'd to pleasance,
Of all comfort having abundance;
This joy and I, I trust, shall never twin —
My heart is set upon a lusty pin.

I pray to Venus of good continuance
Since she hath set me in the way of ease;
My hearty service with my attendance
So to continue it ever I may please;
Thus voiding from all pensful disease,
Now stand I whole far from all grievance —
I pray to Venus of good continuance.

For I rejoice the case that I am in,
My gladness is such that giveth me no pain,
And so to sorrow never shall I blynne,
And though I would I may not me refrain;
My heart and I so set 'tis certain
We shall never slake, but ever new begin —
For I rejoice the case that I am in.

Deliver'd from sorrow, annex'd to pleasance,
That all my joy I set as aught of right,
To please as after my simple suffisance
To me the goodliest, most beauteous in sight;
A very lantern to all other light,
Most to my comfort on her remembrance —
Deliver'd from sorrow, annex'd to pleasance.

Of all comfort having abundance,
As when that I think that goodlihead
Of that most feminine and meek countenance
Very mirror and star of womanhead;
Whose right good fame so large abroad doth spread,
Full glad for me to have recognisance —
Of all comfort having abundance.

This joy and I, I trust, shall never twin,
So that I am so far forth in the trace,
My joys be double where others' are but thin,
For I am stably set in such a place,
Where beauty 'creaseth and ever willeth grace,
Which is full famous and born of noble kin —
This joy and I, I trust, shall never twin.

ANNE BOLEYN (OR BULLEN)

(1507–1536, British)

———

Cruel Spite

Defiléd is my name full sore,
  Through cruel spite and false report,
That I may say for evermore,
  Farewell, my joy! adieu comfórt!

For wrongfully ye judge of me, —
  Unto my fame a mortal wound.
Say what ye list, it will not be;
  Ye seek for that can not be found.

QUEEN ELIZABETH I

(1533–1603, British)

Self and the Otherself

I grieve; and dare not show my discontent!
I love; and yet am forced to seem to hate!
I do; yet dare not say, I ever meant!
I seem stark mute; but inwardly do prate!
I am, and not; I freeze and yet am burned;
Since from myself, my otherself I turned!

My care is like my shadow in the sun;
Follows me flying! flies, when I pursue it!
Stands and lies by me! doth what I have done!
This too familiar Care doth make me rue it!
Nor means I find, to rid him from my breast,
Till by the end of things, it be supprest.

Some gentler Passions slide into my mind;
For I am soft, and made of melting snow.
Or be more cruel, Love! and so be kind:
Let me, or float, or sink! be high, or low!
Or let me live with some more sweet content;
Or die! and so forget what Love e'er meant.

MARY STUART
Queen of Scots
(1542–1587, British)

———

Unfinished Sonnet

O you High Gods, have pity, and let me find
   Somehow some incontestable way to prove
   (So that he *must* believe in it) my love
And this unwavering constancy of mind!
Alas, he rules already with no let
   A body and a heart which must endure
   Pain and dishonour in a life unsure,
The obloquy of friends and worse things yet.

   For him I would account as nothing those
   Whom I named friends, and put my faith in foes:
For him I'd let the round world perish, I
   Who have hazarded both conscience and good name,
And, to advance him, happily would die. . . .
   What's left to prove my love always the same?

ANNE HOWARD
Duchess of Arundel
(1557–1630, British)

———

Elegy on the Death of Her Husband

In sad and ashy weeds I sigh,
   I groan, I pine, I mourn;
My oaten yellow reeds
   I all to jet and ebon turn.
My wat'ry eyes, like winter's skies,
   My furrowed cheeks o'erflow.
All heavens know why men mourn as I,
   And who can blame my woe?

In sable robes of night my days
   Of joy consumed be;
My sorrow sees no light;
   My lights through sorrow nothing see:
For now my sun his course hath run,
   And from his sphere doth go,
To endless bed of soldered lead,
   And who can blame my woe?

My flocks I now forsake, that so
　My sheep my grief may know;
The lilies loath to take
　That since his death presum'd to grow.
I envy air because it dare
　Still breathe, and he not so;
Hate earth, that doth entomb his youth,
　And who can blame my woe?

Not I, poor I alone — (alone
　How can this sorrow be?)
Not only men make moan, but
　More than men make moan with me:
The gods of greens, the mountain queens,
　The fairy circles row,
The muses nine, and powers divine,
　Do all condole my woe.

MARY SIDNEY HERBERT
Countess of Pembroke
(1561–1621, British)

———

If Ever Hapless Woman Had a Cause

If ever hapless woman had a cause
   To breathe her plaints into the open air,
And never suffer inward grief to pause,
   Or seek her sorrow-shaken soul's repair:
Then I, for I have lost my only brother,
Whose like this age can scarcely yield another.

Come therefore, mournful Muses, and lament;
   Forsake all wanton pleasing motions;
Bedew your cheeks. Still shall my tears be spent,
   Yet still increased with inundations.
For I must weep, since I have lost my brother,
Whose like this age can scarcely yield another.

The cruel hand of murder cloyed with blood
   Lewdly deprived him of his mortal life.
Woe the death-attended blades that stood
   In opposition 'gainst him in the strife
Wherein he fell, and where I lost a brother,
Whose like this age can scarcely yield another.

Then unto Grief let me a temple make,
    And, mourning, daily enter Sorrow's ports,
Knock on my breast, sweet brother, for thy sake.
    Nature and love will both be my consorts,
And help me aye to wail my only brother,
Whose like this age can scarcely yield another.

EMILIA LANIER

(1569–1645, British)

———

from *Eves Apologie*

Till now your indiscretion sets us free
And makes our former fault much less appeare;
Our Mother *Eve*, who tasted of the Tree,
Giving to *Adam* what shee held most deare,
Was simply good, and had no powre to see,
The after-comming harme did not appeare:
     The subtile Serpent that our Sex betraide,
     Before our fall so sure a plot had laide.

That undiscerning Ignorance perceav'd
No guile, or craft that was by him intended;
For had she knowne, of what we were bereav'd,
To his request she had not condiscended.
But she (poor soule) by cunning was deceav'd,
No hurt therein her harmelesse Heart intended:
     For she alleadg'd Gods word, which he denies,
     That they should die, but even as Gods, be wise.

And then to lay the fault on Patience backe,
That we (poore women) must endure it all;
We know right well he did discretion lacke,
Beeing not perswaded thereunto at all;
If *Eve* did erre, it was for knowledge sake,
The fruit being faire perswaded him to fall:
     No subtill Serpents falshood did betray him,
     If he would eate it, who had powre to stay him?

[15]

Not *Eve*, whose fault was onely too much love,
Which made her give this present to her Deare,
That what shee tasted, he likewise might prove,
Whereby his knowledge might become more cleare;
He never sought her weakenesse to reprove,
With those sharpe words, which he of God did heare:
    Yet Men will boast of Knowledge, which he tooke
    From *Eves* fair hand, as from a learned Booke.

Then let us have our Libertie againe,
And challendge to your selves no Sov'raigntie;
You came not in the world without our paine,
Make that a barre against your crueltie;
Your fault being greater, why should you disdaine
Our beeing your equals, free from tyranny?
    If one weake woman simply did offend,
    This sinne of yours, hath no excuse, nor end.

ANNE BRADSTREET

(*ca* 1612–1672, American)

——

The Prologue

I am obnoxious to each carping tongue
Who says my hand a needle better fits,
A poet's pen all scorn I should thus wrong,
For such despite they cast on female wits:
If what I do prove well, it won't advance,
They'll say it's stol'n, or else it was by chance.

But sure the antique Greeks were far more mild
Else of our sex, why feigned they those nine
And poesy made Calliope's own child;
So 'mongst the rest they placed the arts divine:
But this weak knot they will full soon untie,
The Greeks did nought, but play the fools and lie.

Let Greeks be Greeks, and women what they are
Men have precedency and still excel,
It is but vain unjustly to wage war;
Men can do best, and women know it well.
Preeminence in all and each is yours;
Yet grant some small acknowledgement of ours.

And oh ye high flown quills that soar the skies,
And ever with your prey still catch your praise,
If e'er you deign these lowly lines your eyes,
Give thyme or parsley wreath, I ask no bays;
This mean and unrefined ore of mine
Will make your glist'ring gold but ore to shine.

MARGARET CAVENDISH
Duchess of Newcastle
(1624–1674, British)

Mirth and Melancholy

Melancholy

Her voice is low and gives a hollow sound;
She hates the light and is in darkness found
Or sits with blinking lamps, or tapers small,
Which various shadows make against the wall.
She loves nought else but noise which discord makes;
As croaking frogs whose dwelling is in lakes;
The raven's hoarse, the mandrake's hollow groan
And shrieking owls which fly i' the night alone;
The tolling bell, which for the dead rings out;
A mill, where rushing waters run about;
The roaring winds, which shake the cedars tall,
Plough up the seas, and beat the rocks withal.
She loves to walk in the still moonshine night,
And in a thick dark grove she takes delight;
In hollow caves, thatched houses, and low cells
She loves to live, and there alone she dwells.

Mirth

I dwell in groves that gilt are with the sun;
Sit on the banks by which clear waters run;
In summers hot down in a shade I lie,
My music is the buzzing of a fly;
I walk in meadows where grows fresh green grass;
In fields where corn is high I often pass;
Walk up the hills, where round I prospects see,
Some bushy woods, and some all champaigns be;
Returning back, I in fresh pastures go,
To hear how sheep do bleat, and cows do low;
In winter cold, when nipping frosts come on,
Then do I live in a small house alone.

KATHERINE PHILIPS
("The Matchless Orinda")
(1631–1664, British)

———

To My Excellent Lucasia, on Our Friendship

I did not live until this time
    Crowned my felicity,
When I could say without a crime,
    I am not thine, but thee.

This carcass breathed, and walked, and slept,
    So that the world believed
There was a soul the motions kept,
    But they were all deceived.

For as a watch by art is wound
    To motion, such was mine:
But never had Orinda found
    A soul till she found thine;

Which now inspires, cures and supplies,
    And guides my darkened breast:
For thou art all that I can prize,
    My joy, my life, my rest.

No bridegroom's nor crown-conqueror's mirth
    To mine compared can be:
They have but pieces of the earth,
    I've all the world in thee.

Then let our flames still light and shine,
    And no false fear control,
As innocent as our design,
    Immortal as our soul.

ANNE KILLIGREW

(1660–1685, British)

————

Upon the Saying That My Verses Were Made by Another

Next heaven, my vows to thee, O sacred Muse!
I offered up, nor didst thou them refuse.

  O queen of verse, said I, if thou'lt inspire,
And warm my soul with thy poetic fire,
No love of gold shall share with thee my heart,
Or yet ambition in my breast have part,
More rich, more noble I will ever hold
The Muse's laurel, than a crown of gold.

An undivided sacrifice I'll lay
Upon thine altar, soul and body pay;
Thou shalt my pleasure, my employment be,
My all I'll make a holocaust to thee.

  Emboldened thus, to fame I did commit
By some few hands, my most unlucky wit.
But ah, the sad effects that from it came!
What ought t'have brought me honour, brought me
      shame!
Like Aesop's painted jay, I seemed to all,
Adorned in plumes, I not my own could call:
Rifled like her, each one my feathers tore,
And, as they thought, unto the owner bore.
My laurels thus another's brow adorned,
My numbers they admired, but me they scorned:

Another's brow, that had so rich a store
Of sacred wreaths that circled it before;
While mine quite lost (like a small stream that ran
Into a vast and boundless ocean,)
Was swallowed up with what it joined, and drowned.
And that abyss yet no accession found.

    Orinda (Albion's and her sex's grace)
Owed not her glory to a beauteous face;
it was her radiant soul that shone within,
Which struck a luster through her outward skin;
That did her lips and cheeks with roses dye,
Advanced her height, and sparkled in her eye.
Nor did her sex at all obstruct her fame,
But higher 'mong the stars it fixed her name;
What she did write, not only all allowed,
But every laurel to her laurel bowed!

    The envious age, only to me alone,
Will not allow what I do write, my own;
But let them rage, and 'gainst a maid conspire,
So deathless numbers from my tuneful lyre
Do ever flow; so, Phoebus, I by thee
Divinely inspired and possessed may be,
I willingly accept Cassandra's fate,
To speak the truth, although believed too late.

ANNE FINCH
Countess of Winchelsea
(1661–1720, British)

———

Trail All Your Pikes

Trail all your pikes, dispirit every drum,
March in a slow procession from afar,
Ye silent, ye dejected, men of war.
Be still the hautboys, and the flute be dumb!
Display no more, in vain, the lofty banner;
For see where on the bier before ye lies
The pale, the fall'n, the untimely sacrifice
To your mistaken shrine, to your false idol Honour.

JANE BRERETON

(17th century, British)

———

On Mr. Nash's Picture at Full Length, Between the Busts of Sir Isaac Newton and Mr. Pope

The old Egyptians hid their wit
   In hieroglyphic dress,
To give men pains to search for it,
   And please themselves with guess.

Moderns, to tread the self-same path
   And exercise our parts,
Place figures in a room at Bath;
   Forgive them, God of Arts!

Newton, if I can judge aright,
   All wisdom doth express,
His knowledge gives mankind new light,
   Adds to their happiness.

Pope is the emblem of true wit,
   The sunshine of the mind;
Read o'er his works for proof of it,
   You'll endless pleasure find.

Nash represents man in the mass,
   Made up of wrong and right;
Sometimes a knave, sometimes an ass,
   Now blunt, and now polite.

The picture, placed the busts between,
   Adds to the thought much strength,
Wisdom and Wit are little seen,
   But Folly's at full length.

"EPHELIA"
(17th century, British)

To Phylocles, Inviting Him to Friendship

Best of thy Sex! if Sacred Friendship can
Dwell in the Bosom of inconstant Man,
As cold and clear as Ice, as Snow unstain'd,
With Love's loose Crimes unsully'd, unprofan'd:

Or you a Woman with that Name dare trust,
And think to Friendship's Ties we can be just:
In a strict League together we'l combine,
And let our Friendship's bright example shine.

We will forget the Difference of Sex,
Nor shall the World's rude Censure us Perplex.
Think Me all Man: my Soul is Masculine,
And Capable of as great Things as Thine.

I can be Gen'rous, Just and Brave,
Secret and Silent as the Grave,
And if I cannot yield Relief,
I'le Sympathize in all thy Grief.

I will not have a Thought from thee I'le hide,
In all my Actions Thou shalt be my Guide;
In every Joy of mine Thou shalt have share,
And I will bear a part in all thy Care.

Why do I vainly Talk of what we'l do?
We'l mix our Souls, you shall be Me, I You;
And both so one it shall be hard to say
Which is Phylocles, which Ephelia.

Our Ties shall be as strong as the Chains of Fate,
Conqu'rors and Kings our Joys shall Emulate;
Forgotten Friendship, held at first Divine,
T'its native Purity we will refine.

ELIZABETH ROWE

(1674–1737, British)

———

To Madam S — — —at the Court

Come, prethee, leave the Courts,
    And range the Fields with me;
A thousand pretty Rural sports
    I'le here invent for thee.

Involv'd in blissful innocence
    Wee'l spend the shining day,
Untoucht with that mean influence
    The duller world obey.

About the flowry Plains wee'l rove
    As gay and unconfin'd
As are inspir'd by thee and love
    The saleys of my mind.

Now seated by a lovely Stream
    Where beauteous Mermaids haunt,
My Song, while William is my Theam,
    Shall them and thee inchant.

Then in some gentle, soft retreat,
    Secure as Venus' Groves,
We'l all the charming things repeat
    That introduc'd our loves.

I'le pluck fresh Garlands for thy brows,
    Sweet as a Zephir's breath,
As fair and well-design'd as those
    The Elisyum Lovers wreath.

And, like those happy Lovers, we,
    As careless and as blest,
Shall, in each others converse, be
    Of the whole world possest.

Then prethee, Phillis, leave the Courts,
    And range the Fields with me,
Since I so many harmless sports
    Can here procure for thee.

LADY MARY WORTLEY MONTAGUE

(1689–1762, British)

———

A Caveat to the Fair Sex

Wife and servant are the same,
But only differ in the name;
For when the fatal knot is ty'd,
Which nothing, nothing can divide;
When she the word *obey* has said,
And man by law supreme is made,
Then all that's kind is laid aside,
And nothing left but state and pride:
Fierce as an Eastern prince he grows,
And all his innate rigour shows;
Then but to look, to laugh, to speak,
Will the nuptial contract break.

Like mutes, the signs alone must make,
And never any freedom take:
But still be govern'd by a nod,
And fear her husband as her god:
Him still must serve, him still obey,
And nothing act, and nothing say,
But what her haughty lord thinks fit,
Who with the power, has all the wit,
Then shun, O shun, that wretched state,
And all the fawning flatterers hate:
Value yourselves; and men despise,
You must be proud, if you'll be wise.

MARY LEAPOR

(1722–1746, British)

———

Upon her Play being returned to her stained with Claret

Welcome, dear Wanderer, once more!
   Thrice welcome to thy native cell!
Within this peaceful humble door
   Let thou and I contented dwell!

But say, O whither hast thou rang'd?
   Why dost thou blush a crimson hue?
Thy fair complexion's greatly chang'd:
   Why, I can scarce believe 'tis you.

Then tell, my son, O tell me, where
   Didst thou contract this sottish dye?
You kept ill company, I fear,
   When distant from your parent's eye.

Was it for this, O graceless child,
   Was it for this you learn'd to spell?
Thy face and credit both are spoil'd;
   Go drown thyself in yonder well.

I wonder how thy time was spent:
   No news (Alas) hast thou to bring?
Hast thou not climb'd the Monument?
   Nor seen the lions, nor the King?

But now I'll keep you here secure:
No more you view the smoky sky:
The court was never made (I'm sure)
For idiots, like thee and I.

ANNA LAETITIA BARBAULD

(1743–1825, British)

The Rights of Women

Yes, injured Woman! rise, assert thy right!
Woman! too long degraded, scorned, opprest;
O born to rule in partial Law's despite,
Resume thy native empire o'er the breast!

Go forth arrayed in panoply divine;
That angel pureness which admits no stain;
Go, bid proud Man his boasted rule resign,
And kiss the golden sceptre of thy reign.

Go, gird thyself with grace; collect thy store
Of bright artillery glancing from afar;
Soft melting tones thy thundering cannon's roar,
Blushes and fears thy magazine of war.

Thy rights are empire: urge no meaner claim, —
Felt, not defiled, and if debated, lost;
Like sacred mysteries, which withheld from fame,
Shunning discussion, are revered the most.

Try all that wit and art suggest to bend
Of thy imperial foe the stubborn knee;
Make treacherous Man thy subject, not thy friend;
Thou mayst command, but never canst be free.

[35]

Awe the licentious, and restrain the rude;
Soften the sullen, clear the cloudy brow:
Be, more than princes' gifts, thy favours sued; —
She hazards all, who will the least allow.

But hope not, courted idol of mankind,
On this proud eminence secure to stay;
Subduing and subdued, thou soon shalt find
Thy coldness soften, and thy pride give way.

Then, then, abandon each ambitious thought,
Conquest or rule thy heart shall feebly move,
In Nature's school, by her soft maxims taught,
That separate rights are lost in mutual love.

FANNY GREVILLE

(18th century, British)

———

Prayer for Indifference

I ask no kind return in love,
  No tempting charm to please;
Far from the heart such gifts remove,
  That sighs for peace and ease.

Nor ease, nor peace, that heart can know,
  That, like the needle true,
Turns at the touch of joy or woe;
  But, turning, trembles too.

Far as distress the soul can wound
  'Tis pain in each degree;
'Tis bliss but to a certain bound,
  Beyond – is agony.

CAROLINA OLIPHANT
Baroness Nairne
(1766–1845, Scottish)

———

Charlie is my Darling

'Twas on a Monday morning,
  Right early in the year,
When Charlie came to our toun,
  The young Chevalier.

    Oh, Charlie is my darling,
      My darling, my darling;
    Oh, Charlie is my darling,
      The young Chevalier.

As he came marching up the street,
  The pipes play'd loud and clear,
And a' the folk came running out
  To meet the Chevalier.

    Oh, Charlie is my darling, . . .

Wi' Hieland bonnets on their heads,
  And claymores bright and clear,
They came to fight for Scotland's right,
  And the young Chevalier.

    Oh, Charlie is my darling, . . .

[38]

They've left their bonnie Hieland hills,
  Their wives and bairnies dear,
To draw the sword for Scotland's lord,
  The young Chevalier.

Oh, Charlie is my darling, . . .

Oh, there were mony beating hearts,
  And mony a hope and fear,
And mony were the prayers put up
  For the young Chevalier.

Oh, Charlie is my darling,
  My darling, my darling;
Oh, Charlie is my darling,
  The young Chevalier.

FELICIA HEMANS

(1793–1835, British)

———

The Homes of England

"Where's the coward that would not dare
To fight for such a land?"
— MARMION

The stately homes of England,
  How beautiful they stand,
Amidst their tall ancestral trees,
  O'er all the pleasant land!
The deer across their greensward bound,
  Through shade and sunny gleam;
And the swan glides past them with the sound
  Of some rejoicing stream.

The merry homes of England!
  Around their hearths by night,
What gladsome looks of household love
  Meet in the ruddy light!
There woman's voice flows forth in song,
  Or childhood's tale is told,
Or lips move tunefully along
  Some glorious page of old.

The blesséd homes of England!
  How softly on their bowers

Is laid the holy quietness
    That breathes from Sabbath hours!
Solemn, yet sweet, the church-bell's chime
    Floats through their woods at morn;
All other sounds, in that still time,
    Of breeze and leaf are born.

The cottage homes of England!
    By thousands on her plains,
They are smiling o'er the silvery brooks,
    And round the hamlet fanes.
Through glowing orchards forth they peep,
    Each from its nook of leaves;
And fearless there the lowly sleep,
    As the bird beneath their eaves.

The free, fair homes of England!
    Long, long, in hut and hall,
May hearts of native proof be reared
    To guard each hallowed wall!
And green for ever be the groves,
    And bright the flowery sod,
Where first the child's glad spirit loves
    Its country and its God!

ELIZABETH BARRETT BROWNING

(1806–1861, British)

---

from *The Cry of the Children*

"φεν, φεν, τι προσδερκεσθε μ ομμασιν, τεκνα;"
— MEDEA
("Do you hear the cry, do you hear the children's cry?"
— MEDEA)

I

Do ye hear the children weeping, O my brothers,
　Ere the sorrow comes with years?
They are leaning their young heads against their mothers,
　And *that* cannot stop their tears.
The young lambs are bleating in the meadows,
　The young birds are chirping in the nest,
The young fawns are playing with the shadows,
　The young flowers are blowing toward the west—
But the young, young children, O my brothers,
　They are weeping bitterly!
They are weeping in the playtime of the others,
　In the country of the free....

Alas, alas, the children! they are seeking
　Death in life, as best to have:
They are binding up their hearts away from breaking,
　With a cerement from the grave.
Go out, children, from the mine and from the city,
　Sing out, children, as the little thrushes do;

Pluck your handfuls of the meadow-cowslips pretty.
    Laugh aloud, to feel your fingers let them through!
But they answer, "Are your cowslips of the meadows
    Like our weeds anear the mine?
Leave us quiet in the dark of the coal-shadows,
    From your pleasures fair and fine!

"For oh," say the children, "we are weary,
    And we cannot run or leap;
If we cared for any meadows, it were merely
    To drop down in them and sleep.
Our knees tremble sorely in the stooping,
    We fall upon our faces, trying to go;
And, underneath our heavy eyelids drooping
    The reddest flower would look as pale as snow.
For, all day, we drag our burden tiring
    Through the coal-dark, underground;
Or, all day, we drive the wheels of iron
    In the factories, round and round.

"For all day the wheels are droning, turning;
    Their wind comes in our faces,
Till our hearts turn, our heads with pulses burning,
    And the walls turn in their places:
Turns the sky in the high window, blank and reeling,
    Turns the long light that drops adown the wall,
Turn the black flies that crawl along the ceiling:
    All are turning, all the day, and we with all.
And all day the iron wheels are droning,
    And sometimes we could pray,
'O ye wheels' (breaking out in a mad moaning),
    "Stop! be silent for today!'" . . .

"Two words indeed, of praying we remember,
    And at midnight's hour of harm.

'Our Father,' looking upward in the chamber,
    We say softly for a charm.
We know no other words except 'Our Father,'
    And we think that, in some pause of angels' song,
God may pluck them with the silence sweet to gather,
    And hold both within his right hand which is strong.
'Our Father!' If He heard us, He would surely
    (For they call Him good and mild)
Answer, smiling down the steep world very purely,
    'Come and rest with me, my child.'

"But, no!" say the children, weeping faster,
    "He is speechless as a stone:
And they tell us, of His image is the master
    Who commands us to work on.
Go to!" say the children, – "up in Heaven,
    Dark, wheel-like, turning clouds are all we find.
Do not mock us; grief has made us unbelieving:
    We look up for God, but tears have made us blind."
Do you hear the children weeping and disproving,
    O my brothers, what ye preach?
For God's possible is taught by his world's loving,
    And the children doubt of each. . . .

They look up with their pale and sunken faces,
    And their look is dread to see,
For they mind you of their angels in high places,
    With eyes turned on Deity.
"How long," they say, "how long, O cruel nation,
    Will you stand, to move the world, on a child's heart, –
Stifle down with a mailéd heel its palpitation,
    And tread onward to your throne amid the mart?

Our blood splashes upward, O goldheaper,
  And your purple shows your path!
But the child's sob in the silence curses deeper
  Than the strong man in his wrath."

CHARLOTTE BRONTË

(1816–1855, British)

Watching and Wishing

Oh, would I were the golden light
  That shines around thee now,
As slumber shades the spotless white
  Of that unclouded brow!
It watches through each changeful dream
  Thy features' varied play;
It meets thy waking eyes' soft gleam
  By dawn – by op'ning day.

Oh, would I were the crimson veil
  Above thy couch of snow,
To dye thy cheek so soft, so pale,
  With my reflected glow!
Oh, would I were the cord of gold
  Whose tassel set with pearls
Just meets the silken cov'ring's fold
  And rests upon thy curls,

Dishevell'd in thy rosy sleep,
  And shading soft thy dreams;
Across their bright and raven sweep
  The golden tassel gleams!
I would be anything for thee,
  My love – my radiant love –
A flower, a bird, for sympathy,
  A watchful star above.

EMILY BRONTË

(1818–1848, British)

———

Remembrance

Cold in the earth, and the deep snow piled above thee!
Far, far removed, cold in the dreary grave!
Have I forgot, my Only Love, to love thee,
Severed at last by Time's all-wearing wave?

Now, when alone, do my thoughts no longer hover
Over the mountains on Angora's shore;
Resting their wings where heath and fern-leaves cover
That noble heart for ever, ever more?

Cold in the earth, and fifteen wild Decembers
From those brown hills have melted into spring —
Faithful indeed is the spirit that remembers
After such years of change and suffering!

Sweet Love of youth, forgive if I forgot thee
While the World's tide is bearing me along:
Sterner desires and darker hopes beset me,
Hopes which obscure but cannot do thee wrong.

No other Sun has lightened up my heaven;
No other Star has ever shone for me;
All my life's bliss from thy dear life was given —
All my life's bliss is in the grave with thee.

But when the days of golden dreams had perished
And even Despair was powerless to destroy,
Then did I learn how existence could be cherished,
Strengthened and fed without the aid of joy;

Then did I check the tears of useless passion,
Weaned my young soul from yearning after thine;
Sternly denied its burning wish to hasten
Down to that tomb already more than mine!

And even yet, I dare not let it languish,
Dare not indulge in Memory's rapturous pain;
Once drinking deep of that divinest anguish,
How could I seek the empty world again?

JULIA WARD HOWE

(1819–1910, American)

———

Battle-Hymn of the Republic

Mine eyes have seen the glory of the coming of the Lord:
He is trampling out the vintage where the grapes of wrath
      are stored;
He hath loosed the fateful lightning of his terrible swift
      sword:
        His truth is marching on.

I have seen Him in the watch-fires of a hundred circling
      camps;
They have builded Him an altar in the evening dews and
      damps;
I can read his righteous sentence by the dim and flaring
      lamps.
        His day is marching on.

I have read a fiery gospel, writ in burnished rows of steel:
"As ye deal with my contemners, so with you my grace
      shall deal;
Let the Hero, born of woman, crush the serpent with his
      heel,
        Since God is marching on."

He has sounded forth the trumpet that shall never call
      retreat;
He is sifting out the hearts of men before his judgment-
      seat:

Oh! be swift, my soul, to answer Him! be jubilant, my
feet!
Our God is marching on.

In the beauty of the lilies Christ was born across the sea,
With a glory in his bosom that transfigures you and me:
As he died to make men holy, let us die to make men free,
While God is marching on.

EMILY DICKINSON

(1830–1886, American)

———

(#505)

I would not paint — a picture —
I'd rather be the One
It's bright impossibility
To dwell — delicious — on —
And wonder how the fingers feel
Whose rare — celestial — stir —
Evokes so sweet a Torment —
Such sumptuous — Despair —

I would not talk, like Cornets —
I'd rather be the One
Raised softly to the Ceilings —
And out, and easy on —
Through Villages of Ether —
Myself endued Balloon
By but a lip of Metal —
The pier to my Pontoon —

Nor would I be a Poet —
It's finer — own the Ear —
Enamored — impotent — content —
The License to revere,
A privilege so awful
What would the Dower be,
Had I the Art to stun myself
With Bolts of Melody!

CHRISTINA ROSSETTI

(1830–1894, British)

———

A Birthday

My heart is like a singing bird
   Whose nest is in a watered shoot;
My heart is like an apple-tree
   Whose boughs are bent with thickset fruit;
My heart is like a rainbow shell
   That paddles in a halcyon sea;
My heart is gladder than all these
   Because my love is come to me.

Raise me a dais of silk and down;
   Hang it with vair and purple dyes;
Carve it in doves and pomegranates,
   And peacocks with a hundred eyes;
Work it in gold and silver grapes,
   In leaves and silver fleurs-de-lys;
Because the birthday of my life
   Is come, my love is come to me.

ALICE MEYNELL

(1847–1922, British)

The Rainy Summer

There's much afoot in heaven and earth this year;
   The winds hunt up the sun, hunt up the moon,
Trouble the dubious dawn, hasten the drear
   Height of a threatening noon.

No breath of boughs, no breath of leaves, of fronds,
   May linger or grow warm; the trees are loud;
The forest, rooted, tosses in her bonds,
   And strains against the cloud.

No scents may pause within the garden-fold;
   The rifled flowers are cold as ocean-shells;
Bees, humming in the storm, carry their cold
   Wild honey to cold cells.

EMMA LAZARUS

(1849–1887, American)

―――

The New Colossus

Not like the brazen giant of Greek fame,
With conquering limbs astride from land to land;
Here at our sea-washed, sunset gates shall stand
A mighty woman with a torch, whose flame
Is the imprisoned lightning, and her name
Mother of Exiles. From her beacon-hand
Glows world-wide welcome; her mild eyes command
The air-bridged harbor that twin cities frame.
"Keep ancient lands, your storied pomp!" cries she
With silent lips. "Give me your tired, your poor,
Your huddled masses yearning to breathe free,
The wretched refuse of your teeming shore.
Send these, the homeless, tempest-tost to me,
I lift my lamp beside the golden door!"

ELLA WHEELER WILCOX

(1850–1919, American)

Delilah

In the midnight of darkness and terror,
When I would grope nearer to God,
With my back to a record of error
And the highway of sin I have trod,
There come to me shapes I would banish —
The shapes of the deeds I have done;
And I pray and I plead till they vanish —
All vanish and leave me, save one.

That one, with a smile like the splendor
Of the sun in the middle-day skies —
That one, with a spell that is tender —
That one with a dream in her eyes —
Cometh close, in her rare Southern beauty,
Her languor, her indolent grace;
And my soul turns its back on its duty,
To live in the light of her face.

She touches my cheek, and I quiver —
I tremble with exquisite pains;
She sighs — like an overcharged river
My blood rushes on through my veins;
She smiles — and in mad-tiger fashion,
As a she-tiger fondles her own,
I clasp her with fierceness and passion,
And kiss her with shudder and groan.

O ghost of dead sin unrelenting,
Go back to the dust, and the sod!
Too dear and too sweet for repenting,
Ye stand between me and my God.
If I, by the Throne, should behold you,
Smiling up with those eyes loved so well,
Close, close in my arms I would fold you,
And drop with you down to sweet Hell!

MARY ELIZABETH COLERIDGE

(1861–1907, British)

———

Doubt

Two forms of darkness are there. One is Night,
When I have been an animal, and feared
I knew not what, and lost my soul, nor dared
Feel aught save hungry longing for the light.
And one is Blindness. Absolute and bright,
The Sun's rays smote me till they masked the Sun;
The Light itself was by the light undone;
The day was filled with terrors and affright.

Then did I weep, compassionate of those
Who see no friend in God—in Satan's host no foes.

CHARLOTTE MEW

(1870–1928, British)

———

The Trees Are Down

—and he cried with a loud voice:
Hurt not the earth, neither the sea,
nor the trees —
— REVELATION

They are cutting down the great plane-trees at the end of
    the gardens.
For days there has been the grate of the saw, the swish of
    the branches as they fall,
The crash of trunks, the rustle of trodden leaves,
With the "Whoops" and the "Whoas," the loud common
    talk, the loud common laughs of the men, above it
    all.

I remember one evening of a long past Spring
Turning in at a gate, getting out of a cart, and finding
    a large dead rat in the mud of the drive.
I remember thinking: alive or dead, a rat was a god-
    forsaken thing,
But at least, in May, that even a rat should be alive.

The week's work here is as good as done. There is just
    one bough
  On the roped bole, in the fine grey rain,
    Green and high

And lonely against the sky.
    (Down now! –)
And but for that,
If an old dead rat
Did once, for a moment, unmake the Spring, I might
    never have thought of him again.

It is not for a moment the Spring is unmade to-day;
These were great trees, it was in them from root to stem:
When the men with the "Whoops" and the "Whoas" have
    carted the whole of the whispering loveliness away
Half the Spring, for me, will have gone with them.

It is going now, and my heart has been struck with the
    hearts of the planes;
Half my life it has beat with these, in the sun, in the rains,
  In the March wind, the May breeze,
In the great gales that came over to them across the roofs
    from the great seas.

  There was only a quiet rain when they were dying;
  They must have heard the sparrows flying,
And the small creeping creatures in the earth where they
    were lying –
  But I, all day, I heard an angel crying:
  "Hurt not the trees."

WILLA CATHER

(1873–1947, American)

The Tavern

In the tavern of my heart
   Many a one has sat before,
Drunk red wine and sung a stave,
   And, departing, come no more.
When the night was cold without,
   And the ravens croaked of storm,
They have sat them at my hearth,
   Telling me my house was warm.

As the lute and cup went round,
   They have rhymed me well in lay; —
When the hunt was on at morn,
   Each, departing, went his way.
On the walls, in compliment,
   Some would scrawl a verse or two,
Some have hung a willow branch,
   Or a wreath of corn-flowers blue.

Ah! my friend, when thou dost go,
   Leave no wreath of flowers for me;
Not pale daffodils nor rue,
   Violets nor rosemary.
Spill the wine upon the lamps,
   Tread the fire, and bar the door;
So despoil the wretched place,
   None will come forevermore.

AMY LOWELL

(1874–1925, American)

———

The Lonely Wife

The mist is thick. On the wide river, the water-plants float
   smoothly.
No letters come; none go.
There is only the moon, shining through the clouds of a
   hard, jade-green sky,
Looking down at us so far divided, so anxiously apart.
All day, going about my affairs, I suffer and grieve, and
   press the thought of you closely to my heart.
My eyebrows are locked in sorrow, I cannot separate
   them.
Nightly, nightly, I keep ready half the quilt,
And wait for the return of that divine dream which is my
   Lord.

Beneath the quilt of the Fire-Bird, on the bed of the
   Silver-Crested Love-Pheasant,
Nightly, nightly, I drowse alone.
The red candles in the silver candlesticks melt, and the
   wax runs from them,
As the tears of your so Unworthy One escape and
   continue constantly to flow.
A flower face endures but a short season,
Yet still he drifts along the river Hsiao and the river
   Hsiang.

As I toss on my pillow, I hear the cold, nostalgic sound of
the water-clock:
Shêng! Shêng! it drips, cutting my heart in two.

I rise at dawn. In the Hall of Pictures
They come and tell me that the snow-flowers are falling.
The reed-blind is rolled high, and I gaze at the beautiful,
glittering, primeval snow,
Whitening the distance, confusing the stone steps and the
courtyard.
The air is filled with its shining, it blows far out like the
smoke of a furnace.
The grass-blades are cold and white, like jade girdle
pendants.
Surely the Immortals in Heaven must be crazy with wine
to cause such disorder,
Seizing the white clouds, crumpling them up, destroying
them.

after Li Po

GERTRUDE STEIN

(1874–1946, American)

———

from *Winning His Way*

What is poetry. This. Is poetry.
Delicately formed. And pleasing. To the eye.
What is fame. Fame is. The care of. Their. Share.
And so. It. Rhymes better.
A pleasure in wealth. Makes. Sunshine.
And a. Pleasure. In sunshine. Makes wealth.
They will manage very well. As they. Please. Them.
What is fame. They are careful. Of awakening. The.
    Name.
And so. They. Wait. With oxen. More. Than one.
They speak. Of matching. Country oxen. And.
They speak. Of waiting. As if. They. Had won.
By their. Having. Made. A pleasure. With. Their.
May they. Make it. Rhyme. All. The time.
This is. A pleasure. In poetry. As often. As. Ever.
They will. Supply it. As. A measure.
Be why. They will. Often. Soften.
As they may. As. A. Treasure.

ANNA HEMPSTEAD BRANCH

(1875–1937, American)

———

from *In the Beginning Was the Word*

It took me ten days
To read the Bible through,
Then I saw what I saw,
And I knew what I knew. . . .

For a great wind blows
Through Ezekiel and John,
They are all one flesh
That the Spirit breathes upon.

And suddenly the words
Seemed to quicken and to shine;
They glowed like the bread,
They purpled like the wine.

Like bread that had been wheat
In a thousand ample plains,
Sown and harvested by men
From the suns — from the rains.

Like wine that had been grapes
In a thousand vineyards strong —
That was trampled by men's feet
With a shout, with a song.

Like the Bread, like the Wine,
That we eat with one accord —
The body and the blood
Of the supper of the Lord....

For a great wind blows
Through Ezekiel and John,
They are all one flesh
That the Spirit breathes upon.

The Book felt like flesh,
It would breathe — it would sing —
It would throb beneath my hand
Like a bird, like a wing.

And my flesh was in the Book,
And its blood was in me;
I could feel it throb within,
As plain as it could be.

I was filled with its powers,
And I cried all alone,
"The Lord is in the tomb,
And my body is the stone."

And I swung one side
When the ghostly power began.
Then the Book stood up —
And I saw it was a Man.

For a great wind blows
Through Ezekiel and John.
They are all one flesh
That the Spirit breathes upon.

It took me ten days
To read the Bible through —
Then I saw what I saw,
And I knew what I knew.

SARAH CLEGHORN

(1876–1959, American)

———

(Quatrain)

The golf links lie so near the mill
That almost every day
The laboring children can look out
And see the men at play.

MINA LOY

(1882–1966, American)

The Black Virginity

Baby Priests
On green sward
Yew-closed
Scuttle to sunbeams
Silk beaver
Rhythm of redemption
Fluttering of Breviaries

Fluted black silk cloaks
Hung square from shoulders
Truncated juvenility
Uniform segregation
Union in severity
Modulation
Intimidation
Pride of misapprehended preparation
Ebony statues training for immobility
Anaemic-jawed
Wise saw to one another

Prettily the little ones
Gesticulate benignly upon one another in the sun buzz –
Finger and thumb circles postulate pulpits
Profiles forsworn to Donatello
Munching tall talk vestral shop
Evangelical snobs

Uneasily dream
In hermetically sealed dormitories
Not of me or you Sister Saraminta
Of no more or less
Than the fit of the Pope's miters

It is an old religion that put us in our places
Here I am in lilac print
Preposterously no less than the world flesh and devil
Having no more idea what those are
What I am
Than Baby Priests of what "He" is
or they are —
Messianic mites tripping measured latin ring-a-roses
Subjugated adolescence
Retracing lost steps to furling of Breviaries
In broiling shadows
The last with apostolic lurch
Tries for a high-hung fruit
And misses
Anyway it is inedible

It is always thus
In the Public Garden

    Parallel lines
An old man
Eyeing a white muslin girls' school
And all this
As pleasant as bewildering
    Would not eventually meet

I am forever bewildered
Old men are often grown greedy —

What nonsense
It is noon

And salvation's seedlings
Are headed off for the refectory

ELINOR WYLIE

(1885–1928, American)

Velvet Shoes

Let us walk in the white snow
   In a soundless space;
With footsteps quiet and slow,
   At a tranquil pace,
   Under veils of white lace.

I shall go shod in silk,
   And you in wool,
White as a white cow's milk,
   More beautiful
   Than the breast of a gull.

We shall walk through the still town
   In a windless peace;
We shall step upon white down,
   Upon silver fleece,
   Upon softer than these.

We shall walk in velvet shoes:
   Wherever we go
Silence will fall like dews
   On white silence below.
   We shall walk in the snow.

H.D.

(1886–1961, American)

———

Helen

All Greece hates
the still eyes in the white face,
the lustre as of olives
where she stands,
and the white hands.

All Greece reviles
the wan face when she smiles,
hating it deeper still
when it grows wan and white,
remembering past enchantments
and past ills.

Greece sees unmoved,
God's daughter, born of love,
the beauty of cool feet
and slenderest knees,
could love indeed the maid,
only if she were laid,
white ash amid funereal cypresses.

FRANCES CORNFORD

(1886–1960, British)

——

The New-Born Baby's Song

When I was twenty inches long,
I could not hear the thrushes' song;
The radiance of morning skies
Was most displeasing to my eyes.

For loving looks, caressing words,
I cared no more than sun or birds;
But I could bite my mother's breast,
And that made up for all the rest.

MARIANNE MOORE

(1887–1972, American)

———

Poetry

I, too, dislike it: there are things that are important
      beyond all this fiddle.
  Reading it, however, with a perfect contempt for it, one
        discovers in
  it after all, a place for the genuine.
     Hands that can grasp, eyes
     that can dilate, hair that can rise
        if it must, these things are important not because a

high-sounding interpretation can be put upon them but
      because they are
  useful. When they become so derivative as to become
        unintelligible,
  the same thing may be said for all of us, that we
    do not admire what
    we cannot understand: the bat
     holding on upside down or in quest of something to

eat, elephants pushing, a wild horse taking a roll, a tireless
      wolf under a tree, the immovable critic twitching
      his skin like a horse that feels a flea, the base-
ball fan, the statistician —
  nor is it valid
    to discriminate against 'business documents and

school-books'; all these phenomena are important. One
    must make a distinction
  however: when dragged into prominence by half poets,
    the result is not poetry,
  nor till the poets among us can be
    'literalists of
    the imagination'—above
      insolence and triviality and can present

for inspection, imaginary gardens with real toads in them,
    shall we have
  it. In the meantime, if you demand on the one hand,
  the raw material of poetry in
    all its rawness and
    that which is on the other hand
      genuine, then you are interested in poetry.

MARY BUTTS

(1890–1937, British)

———

Thinking of Saints and of Petronius Arbithe

Between a toy and a crucifix
Between a joke and a prayer
Lies the Bird-catcher
Who caught the peacock of the world;
The poet the saint the gentleman and the wit
Making these titles tolerable again.

Between a cigarette and a cocktail
Between a spite and a fear
Round a bar
Runs a little boy afraid of his whipped shadow
Tender about his fear.

Between the cocktail and the crucifix
Between the prayer and the fear
Lies the sword.

Between the toy and the cigarette
Between the spite and the joke
Lies the imagination.

Between the bird and the bar is the choice of consolation
Tastes of the gentleman and the *garcon de promenoir.*

Between the tapette and the poet
Between the prayer and the fear
There is time for thought:

[76]

Between the joy-boy and the gentleman
Between the bed and the bar
There is room to move about,

Between the poet and the tapette
Between the grace and the disgrace
There is no choice.

Between the sleeping squirrel in the wood
And the night rat
Lies the shadow, the identity,

(Not because one knelt
By the bed, And the hands
Of the other were wet
With tears shaken out of a young body
Told not to be afraid to learn to play.)

In the shadow the identity lies.

One is the explanation: the Illumination
Of the darkness
Of the other.

Because love is
Because of what love is
love is vision, in extremes
(We who know what love is)
And it is not possible to love
Any people but these.

EDNA ST. VINCENT MILLAY

(1892–1950, American)

———

Justice Denied in Massachusetts

Let us abandon then our gardens and go home
And sit in the sitting-room.
Shall the larkspur blossom or the corn grow under this
      cloud?
Sour to the fruitful seed
Is the cold earth under this cloud,
Fostering quack and weed, we have marched upon but
      cannot conquer;
We have bent the blades of our hoes against the stalks of
      them.

Let us go home, and sit in the sitting-room.
Not in our day
Shall the cloud go over and the sun rise as before,
Beneficent upon us
Out of the glittering bay,
And the warm winds be blown inward from the sea
Moving the blades of corn
With a peaceful sound.
Forlorn, forlorn,
Stands the blue hay-rack by the empty mow.
And the petals drop to the ground,
Leaving the tree unfruited.
The sun that warmed our stooping backs and withered the
      weed uprooted –

We shall not feel it again.
We shall die in darkness, and be buried in the rain.

What from the splendid dead
We have inherited —
Furrows sweet to the grain, and the weed subdued —
See now the slug and the mildew plunder.
Evil does overwhelm
The larkspur and the corn;
We have seen them go under.

Let us sit here, sit still,
Here in the sitting-room until we die;
At the step of Death on the walk, rise and go;
Leaving to our children's children this beautiful doorway,
And this elm,
And a blighted earth to till
With a broken hoe.

August 22, 1927

RUTH PITTER

(1897–1992, British)

———

But for Lust

But for lust we could be friends,
    On each other's necks could weep:
In each other's arms could sleep
    In the calm the cradle lends:

Lends awhile, and takes away.
    But for hunger, but for fear,
Calm could be our day and year
    From the yellow to the grey:

From the gold to the grey hair,
    But for passion we could rest,
But for passion we could feast
    On compassion everywhere.

Even in this night I know
    By the awful living dead,
By this craving tear I shed,
    Somewhere, somewhere it is so.

LOUISE BOGAN

(1897–1970, American)

—

Kept

Time for the wood, the clay,
The trumpery dolls, the toys
Now to be put away:
We are not girls and boys.

What are these rags we twist
Our hearts upon, or clutch
Hard in the sweating fist?
They are not worth so much.

But we must keep such things
Till we at length begin
To feel our nerves their strings,
Their dust, our blood within.

The dreadful painted bisque
Becomes our very cheek.
A doll's heart, faint at risk,
Within our breast grows weak.

Our hand the doll's, our tongue.

Time for the pretty clay,
Time for the straw, the wood.
The playthings of the young
Get broken in the play,
Get broken, as they should.

LÉONIE ADAMS

(1899–1988, American)

———

The Figurehead

This that is washed with weed and pebblestone
Curved once a dolphin's length before the prow,
And I who read the land to which we bore
In its grave eyes, question my idol now,
What cold and marvelous fancy it may keep,
Since the salt terror swept us from our course,
Or if a wisdom later than the storm,
For old green ocean's tinctured it so deep;
And with some reason to me on this strand
The waves, the ceremonial waves have come,
And stooped their barbaric heads, and all flung out
Their glittering arms before them, and are gone,
Leaving the murderous tribute lodged in sand.

JANET LEWIS

(1899–   , American)

———

Remembered Morning

The axe rings in the wood,
And the children come,
Laughing and wet from the river;
And all goes on as it should.
I hear the murmur and hum
Of their morning forever.

The water ripples and slaps
The white boat at the dock;
The fire crackles and snaps.
The little noise of the clock
Goes on and on in my heart,
Of my heart parcel and part.

O happy early stir!
A girl comes out on the porch
And the door slams after her.
She sees the wind in the birch,
And then the running day
Catches her into its way.

HILDEGARDE FLANNER

(1899–1987, American)

———

The Letters of Robert Oppenheimer: Postscript

To forget him! To forget all of him!
To forget the beautiful skull where genius shuddered!
Suffer him to sink into the white sand
Where his mind pierced the stones and the stones
Marvelled. Consider the stones, they fell in two
And the heavens were speechless. Take alarm.
Did he pray – God, do not make your own God
Of me? The Almighty cleft him
Clairvoyant in a desert of peril
And he rose to meet the world's oncoming princes
Riders riding on many wheels, and rose
To smash the pure monolith of the Creator,
And the desert fled, matter fled away,
The century split, East fled under West,
And the planet sickened.

Therefore the cities were demolished,
Therefore the people broke into fire.
No need to proclaim who did it. There were
Others. On him the rage of glory falls,
On him the magnificent O.

Forget him.
On the breast of good he came upon evil,
And the two faces faced and hated.
Forget him again. He was never at peace.

There he goes, goes with his two fatal ones
Linked and torn, by furies torn and linked.
Do not touch him as he passes.
He is immortal, he is poison.

Down the longest labyrinth let him go,
Now the doors are all locked,

        locks locking locks.

STEVIE SMITH

(1902–1971, British)

———

Not Waving but Drowning

Nobody heard him, the dead man,
But still he lay moaning:
I was much further out than you thought
And not waving but drowning.

Poor chap, he always loved larking
And now he's dead
It must have been too cold for him his heart gave way,
They said.

Oh, no no no, it was too cold always
(Still the dead one lay moaning)
I was much too far out all my life
And not waving but drowning.

EVE TRIEM

(1902–1992, American)

———

The Lazarus Carol

And so we are awake.
Again the grave of sleep
Is robbed of Christ the sun.
We who hated our bodies,
Our habits, our shabby names,
Now we must sin no more.

A river of winter sunrise
Like marred pearls or old paper,
Counting the Solstice hours
Flows from the side of a sun
Nailed to a hilltop pine.

We are redeemed for this:
To make choice shall we weep
Without reason, or wake
A dreadful reason for weeping.

Though the nations, ox and lamb
Garlanded with herbs,
Pretend that for a day
They are ruled from Bethlehem,
The nations pile new weapons
To build their hill of worship.
They set a threatening skull
In the straw of the Manger.

Not by nations but in single
Risings are the living dead
Baptized with the day-shine.
Each of us is chosen
For naming and praising the creatures
So lonely in their beauty,
Of the kingdom of creation —
Or for nothing Christ the sun
Had risen to the worlds.

LORINE NIEDECKER

(1903–1970, American)

———

Seven Poems

1

As praiseworthy

the power of breathing (Epictetus)
while we sleep. Add:
to move the parts of the body
without sound

and to float
on a smooth green stream
in a silent boat

2

My mother saw the green tree toad
on the window sill
her first one
since she was young.
We saw it breathe

and swell up round.
My youth is no sure sign

I'll find this kind of thing
tho it does sing.
Let's take it in

I said so grandmother can see
but she could not
it changed to brown
and town
changed us, too.

3

For best work
you ought to put forth
        some effort
        to stand
in north woods
among birch

4

Young in Fall I said: the birds
are at their highest thoughts
of leaving

Middle life said nothing —
grounded
to a livelihood

Old age — a high gabbling gathering
before goodbye
of all we know

5

Smile
    to see the lake
        lay
    the still sky

And
    out for an easy
        make
    the dragonfly

6

Old man who seined
to educate his daughter
sees red Mars rise:
        What lies
behind it?

Cold water business
now starred in Fishes
of dipnet shape
        to ache
thru his arms.

7

You are my friend —
you bring me peaches
and the high bush cranberry
        you carry
my fishpole

you water my worms
you patch my boot
with your mending kit
        nothing in it
but my hand

JOSEPHINE JACOBSEN

(1908–   , American)

———

Gentle Reader

Late in the night when I should be asleep
under the city stars in a small room
I read a poet. A poet: not
a versifier. Not a hot-shot
ethic-monger, laying about
him; not a diary of lying
about in cruel cruel beds, crying.
A poet, dangerous and steep.

O God, it peels me, juices me like a press;
this poetry drinks me, eats me, gut and marrow
until I exist in its jester's sorrow,
until my juices feed a savage sight
that runs along the lines, bright
as beasts' eyes. The rubble splays to dust:
city, book, bed, leaving my ear's lust
saying like Molly, yes, yes, yes, O yes.

KATHLEEN RAINE

(1908–   , British)

The Unloved

I am pure loneliness
I am empty air
I am drifting cloud.

I have no form
I am boundless
I have no rest.

I have no house
I pass through places
I am indifferent wind.

I am the white bird
Flying away from land
I am the horizon.

I am a wave
That will never reach the shore.

I am an empty shell
Cast up on the sand.

I am the moonlight
On the cottage with no roof.

I am the forgotten dead
In the broken vault on the hill.

I am the old man
Carrying his water in a pail.

I am light
Travelling in empty space.

I am a diminishing star
Speeding away
Out of the universe.

MARY BARNARD

(1909–   , American)

Static

I wanted to hear
Sappho's laughter
and the speech of
her stringed shell.

What I heard was
whiskered mumble-
ment of grammarians:

Greek pterodactyls
and Victorian dodos.

ROSALIE MOORE

(1910–   , American)

After the Storm

Along the streaming ground, the wet leaves fit like fish
And shine like talk.
The prints of the xylophone horses
Clang and revise
Their clear and candid marks.

And only a funeral under a tall quartz sky
Can bring us together as steeply
As these oak trees
And this tomb.

All talk seems genuine: the syllables make evident
Their wild, pronounced colonies.

The word is out — a racket of hail and rhyme
Is landing a few Greek letters at a time.

If any have other knowledge of the crime,
Let him speak, lest the privilege harden;
Let us acknowledge
The rains were heavy and the damage severe —

Yet there are times when the uncut universe comes close
And whets like a diamond,
And the useful joy seems near.

And the diamond is odd in its meaning,
It rests like a water-mark,
Is read by the shining door.

MURIEL RUKEYSER

(1913–1980, American)

———

The Poem as Mask

Orpheus

When I wrote of the women in their dances and wildness,
     it was a mask,
on their mountain, god-hunting, singing, in orgy,
it was a mask; when I wrote of the god,
fragmented, exiled from himself, his life, the love gone
     down with song,
it was myself, split open, unable to speak, in exile from
     myself.

There is no mountain, there is no god, there is memory
of my torn life, myself split open in sleep, the rescued
     child
beside me among the doctors, and a word
of rescue from the great eyes.

No more masks! No more mythologies!

Now, for the first time, the god lifts his hand,
the fragments join in me with their own music.

MAY SWENSON

(1913–1989, American)

———

Question

Body my house
my horse my hound
what will I do
when you are fallen

Where will I sleep
How will I ride
What will I hunt

Where can I go
without my mount
all eager and quick
How will I know
in thicket ahead
is danger or treasure
when Body my good
bright dog is dead

How will it be
to lie in the sky
without roof or door
and wind for an eye

With cloud for shift
how will I hide?

GWEN HARWOOD

(1915–   , Australian)

———

Madame Esmerelda's Predictions

Dream and instinct will warn
    the cock against the fox.
Tick-bird and crocodile
    are bound to live in peace.
Step by step behind you
    something will be destroyed.
The glass is clearing. Something
    ancient makes itself known.
My voice is not my own.
    We are in the House of Language.
I see the coming age.
    Good poetry will change.
Bad will be much the same.
    As for yourself: I see
two cloudy people sharing
    a cup, a man and woman.
They have drunk their death. I fear
    your love will not return.

RUTH STONE

(1915–   , American)

———

Curtains

Putting up new curtains,
other windows intrude.
As though it is that first winter in Cambridge
when you and I had just moved in.
Now cold borscht alone in a bare kitchen.

What does it mean if I say this years later?

Listen, last night
I am on a crying jag
with my landlord, Mr. Tempesta.
I sneaked in two cats.
He screams NO PETS! NO PETS!
I become my Aunt Virginia,
proud but weak in the head.
I remember Anna Magnani.
I throw a few books. I shout.
He wipes his eyes and opens his hands.
OK OK keep the dirty animals
but no nails in the walls.
We cry together.
I am so nervous, he says.

I want to dig you up and say, look,
it's like the time, remember,
when I ran into our living room naked
to get rid of that fire inspector.

See what you miss by being dead?

JUDITH WRIGHT

(1915–   , Australian)

———

Australia 1970

Die, wild country, like the eaglehawk,
dangerous till the last breath's gone,
clawing and striking. Die
cursing your captor through a raging eye.

Die like the tigersnake
that hisses such pure hatred from its pain
as fills the killer's dreams
with fear like suicide's invading stain.

Suffer, wild country, like the ironwood
that gaps the dozer-blade.
I see your living soil ebb with the tree
to naked poverty.

Die like the soldier-ant
mindless and faithful to your million years.
Though we corrupt you with our torturing mind,
stay obstinate; stay blind.

For we are conquerors and self-poisoners
more than scorpion or snake
and dying of the venoms that we make
even while you die of us.

I praise the scoring drought, the flying dust,
the drying creek, the furious animal,
that they oppose us still;
that we are ruined by the thing we kill.

GWENDOLYN BROOKS

(1917–   , American)

———

We Real Cool

The Pool Players.
Seven at the Golden Shovel

We real cool. We
Left school. We

Lurk late. We
Strike straight. We

Sing sin. We
Thin gin. We

Jazz June. We
Die soon.

MURIEL SPARK

(1918–   , Scottish)

———

Going up to Sotheby's

This was the wine. It stained the top of the page
when she knocked over the glass accidentally. A pity,
        she said,
to lose that drop. For the wine was a treat.
Here's a coffee-cup ring, and another. He preferred
        coffee to tea.
Some pages re-written entirely, scored through,
        cancelled over and over
on this, his most important manuscript.

That winter they took a croft in Perthshire,
living on oats and rabbits bought for a few pence
        from the madman.
The children thrived, and she got them to school
        daily, mostly by trudge.
He was glad to get the children out of the way, but
        always felt cold
while working on his book. This
is his most important manuscript, completed 1929.
'Children, go and play outside. Your father's trying
        to work.
But keep away from the madman's house.'
He looked up from his book. 'There's nothing
wrong with the madman.' Which was true.

She typed out the chapters in the afternoons. He
        looked happily at her.
He worked best late at night.
'Aren't you ever coming to bed? I often wonder,
are you married to me or to your bloody book?'
A smudge on the page, still sticky after all these years.
Something greasy on the last page.
This is that manuscript, finished in the late spring,
crossed-out, dog-eared; this, the original,
passed through several literary hands while
the pages she had typed were at the publishers'.
One personage has marked a passage with red ink,
has written in the margin, 'Are you *sure?*'

Five publishers rejected it in spite of recommendations.
The sixth decided to risk his pounds sterling down
        the drain
for the sake of prestige. The author was a difficult
        customer. However,
they got the book published at last.
Her parents looked after the children while the couple
        went to France
for a short trip. This bundle of paper, the original
        manuscript,
went into a fibre trunk, got damp into it, got mouldy
        and furled.
It took fifteen more years for him to make his reputation,
by which time the children had grown up, Agnes as a
secretary at the BBC, Leo as a teacher.

The author died in '48, his wife, in '68.
Agnes and Leo married and begat.
And now the grandchildren are selling the manuscript.
Bound and proud, documented and glossed
by scholars of the land, smoothed out

and precious, these leaves of paper
are going up to Sotheby's. The wine-stained,
stew-stained and mould-smelly papers are
going up to Sotheby's. They occupy the front seat
of the Renault, beside the driver.
They are a national event. They are going up
to make their fortune at last,
which once were so humble, tattered, and so truly
        working class.

ELMA MITCHELL

(1919–   , Scottish)

———

Thoughts after Ruskin

Women reminded him of lilies and roses.
Me they remind rather of blood and soap,
Armed with a warm rag, assaulting noses,
Ears, neck, mouth and all the secret places:

Armed with a sharp knife, cutting up liver,
Holding hearts to bleed under a running tap,
Gutting and stuffing, pickling and preserving,
Scalding, blanching, broiling, pulverising,
— All the terrible chemistry of their kitchens.

Their distant husbands lean across mahogany
And delicately manipulate the market,
While safe at home, the tender and the gentle
Are killing tiny mice, dead snap by the neck,
Asphyxiating flies, evicting spiders,
Scrubbing, scouring aloud, disturbing cupboards,
Committing things to dustbins, twisting, wringing,
Wrists red and knuckles white and fingers puckered,
Pulpy, tepid. Steering screaming cleaners
Around the snags of furniture, they straighten
And haul out sheets from under the incontinent
And heavy old, stoop to importunate young,
Tugging, folding, tucking, zipping, buttoning,
Spooning in food, encouraging excretion,
Mopping up vomit, stabbing cloth with needles,

Contorting wool around their knitting needles,
Creating snug and comfy on their needles. . . .

And when all's over, off with overalls,
Quickly consulting clocks, they go upstairs,
Sit and sigh a little, brushing hair,
And somehow find, in mirrors, colours, odours,
Their essences of lilies and of roses.

HILDA MORLEY

(1919–   , American)

It Is the Living

It is the living who cannot
live without the dead,
                    who wish them
back,
        who need their presences,
their hands,
                as Orpheus
held her hand, Eurydice's,
to lead her
back to earth out of
the gulf of Hades,
                    as I
need yours
            It is not so much
the dead
        who need us
now
    (as we think they do)
                        & that reconciliation
we long for, that knowledge
of each other to the uttermost,
which could assuage us,
                    they are
one step beyond it & suffer us
to long for them.

If they could
return, it would be out of
patience with us merely: their need to
console us. For somehow an indifference
possesses them, for all their tenderness
& they see beyond us,
                              even if
what they see seems to us
nothing

AMY CLAMPITT

(1920–1994, American)

———

Dodona: Asked of the Oracle

The female body, its creases and declivities
leading to the sacred opening, the hollow
whose precincts, here, neither seduce nor threaten:
bee-hum, birdsong, side-oats' leaning awns,
the blowing grasses (one vivid
lizard flickers on gray stone,
is gone); the drifting
down of poplars; harebells,
convolvulus. The triumph-song,
far off, of strutting cocks
no threat, merely ridiculous. Olympus
a mountain range away: huge valleys
charged with gargantuan
foreshadowings, new-minted
laser glints of force.
                                        From such bluster
was this once a place of refuge? Before Dione,
the dim earlier consort, gave place
to bitchy Hera (who for her nagging
had, of course, good cause),
was there a season when
the unraised voice, attuned
to civic reticence by whisperings
among totemic oak leaves,
might gain a hearing?

[113]

                        Or did that wounded,
melismatic howl, heard now from
the taxicab cassette, or filtered
through the heat of the debate
above the tric-trac — whether
of shaman, priest, muezzin
or lying, half-self-deceived seducer —
countervail: this siren
tremor, male, ancient,
mindless, that raises
Armageddons from within the doddering
sheep run of politics — this echo
of recesses deeper, even, than
the archetypal cleft of sex?

ROSEMARY DOBSON

(1920–   , Australian)

———

The Three Fates

At the instant of drowning he invoked the three sisters.
It was a mistake, an aberration, to cry out for
life everlasting.

He came up like a cork and back to the river-bank,
put on his clothes in reverse order,
returned to the house.

He suffered the enormous agonies of passion
writing poems from the end backwards,
brushing away tears that had not yet fallen.

Loving her wildly as the day regressed towards morning
he watched her swinging in the garden, growing younger,
barefoot, straw-hatted.

And when she was gone and the house and the swing and
        daylight
there was an instant's pause before it began all over,
the reel unrolling towards the river.

MONA VAN DUYN

(1921–   , American)

———

from *Three Valentines to the Wide World*

III

"Your yen two wol slee me sodenly;
I may the beautee of hem not sustene."

—MERCILES BEAUTE

When, in the middle of my life, the earth stalks me
with sticks and stones, I fear its merciless beauty.
This morning a bird woke me with a four-note outcry,
and cried out eighteen times. With the shades down,
     sleepy
as I was, I recognized his agony.
It resembles ours. With one more heave, the day
sends us a generous orb and lets us see
all sights lost when we lie down finally.

And if, in the middle of her life, some beauty falls on
a girl, who turns under its swarm to astonished woman,
then, into that miraculous buzzing, stung
in the lips and eyes without mercy, strangers may run.
An untended power—I pity her and them.
It is late, late; haste! says the falling moon,
as blinded they stand and smart till the fever's done
and blindly she moves, wearing her furious weapon.

Beauty is merciless and intemperate.
Who, turning this way and that, by day, by night,
still stands in the heart-felt storm of its benefit,
will plead in vain for mercy, or cry, "Put out
the lovely eyes of the world, whose rise and set
move us to death!" And never will temper it,
but against that rage slowly may learn to pit
love and art, which are compassionate.

CONSTANCE URDANG

(1922–   , American)

———

A Life You Might Say You Might Live

You might call it *a road*,
This track that swerves across the dry field,
And you might call this alley a *street*,
This alley that stumbles downhill between the high walls
And what you might call *doorways*, these black mouths
That open into caves you might call *houses;*
And if you turned at the corner
Into a narrower alley, you might still call it
Going home, and when you got to the place
Where it dwindles to a footpath, and you kept on walking
You would finally come to what you might call *the threshold*
Of a life, of what you might call *your life.*

MARIE PONSOT

(1922–   , American)

———

Communion of Saints:
The Poor Bastard under the Bridge

The arrows of the narrow moon flock down direct
Into that looking heart by Seine walls unprotected.
Moonward the eyes of that hurt head still will
Stare and scarcely see the moonlight spill
Because black Notre Dame between her towers
Strikes home to him the third of this day's hours
And he, now man, heaped cold afaint
Below the Pont Marie will, with a shout,
Enlist among the triumphant when Poor Saint
Julien's bells will clock out
Four.
          In his rags, unchapleted, almost astray
Among the dead packed all immaculate away
Under the city, he awaits his sentry
The four o'clock moon to warrant for his entry
                    o and pure
The pure in children's ranks by bells immured
In gowns of light will singing telling rise
Unfold their arms impelled without surprise
Will lift up flowered laurel, will walk out
Among their golden singing like a victor's shout
To their triumphant heaven's golden ringing brim
And welcome welcome welcome him.

DENISE LEVERTOV

(1923–   , American)

———

Poet and Person

I send my messages ahead of me.
You read them, they speak to you
in siren tongues, ears of flame
spring from your heads to take them.

When I arrive, you love me,
for I sing those messages you've
learned by heart, and bring,
as housegifts, new ones. You hear

yourselves in them,
self after self. Your solitudes
utter their runes, your own
voices begin to rise in your throats.

But soon you love me less.
I brought with me
too much, too many laden coffers,
the panoply of residence,

improper to a visit.
Silks and furs, my enormous wings,
my crutches, and my spare crutches,
my desire to please, and worse—

my desire to judge what is right.

I take up
so much space.
You are living on what you can find,
you don't want charity, and you can't
support lingering guests.

When I leave, I leave
alone, as I came.

LISEL MUELLER

(1924–   , American)

——

Romantics

Johannes Brahms and Clara Schumann

The modern biographers worry
"how far it went," their tender friendship.
They wonder just what it means
when he writes he thinks of her constantly,
his guardian angel, beloved friend.
The modern biographers ask
the rude, irrelevant question
of our age, as if the event
of two bodies meshing together
establishes the degree of love,
forgetting how softly Eros walked
in the nineteenth century, how a hand
held overlong or a gaze anchored
in someone's eyes could unseat a heart,
and nuances of address not known
in our egalitarian language
could make the redolent air
tremble and shimmer with the heat
of possibility. Each time I hear
the Intermezzi, sad
and lavish in their tenderness,
I imagine the two of them
sitting in a garden

among late-blooming roses
and dark cascades of leaves,
letting the landscape speak for them,
leaving us nothing to overhear.

MAXINE KUMIN

(1925–   , American)

———

Getting the Message

God, the rabbis tell us, never assigns
exalted office to a man until
He has tested his mettle in small things.
So it is written in the *Midrash*
that when a lamb escaped the flock Moses
came upon it at a brook drinking its fill
and said, I would have taken thee in my arms
and carried thee thither had I known thy thirst
whereupon a Heavenly Voice warmly
resounded, *As thou livest thou art fit.*

Divine election's scary. The burning bush
might have been brightened by St. Elmo's fire
according to *The Interpreter's One-Volume
Commentary.* The slopes of Exodus,
scrub growth close-cropped by tough horned herds
of Jacob's sheep (now prized as an heirloom breed)
lack treetops, mountain peaks or spires
that might discharge electrical ghost-plumes.
St Elmo's seems less science than the desire
of modern exegetes to damp the flame.

I like my Bible tales, like Scotch, straight up
incontrovertible as Dante's trip
through seven circles, Milton's map
of Paradise or Homer's wine-dark epic.

On such a stage there falls a scrim between
text and critique where bursts of light may crack
and dance as if on masts of sailing ships
and heavenly voices leap from alp to plain.
In Sunday School I shivered at God's command:
Take off thy shoes, thou stand'st on holy ground

and lay awake in the hot clutch of faith
yearning yet fearful that the Lord might speak
to me in my bed or naked in my bath.
I didn't know how little risk I ran
of being asked to set my people free
of fording some metaphorical Red Sea
with a new-sprung Pharaoh raging at my back.
I didn't know the patriarchy that spared me
fame had named me chattel, handmaiden.
God's angels looked me over but flew by.

I like to think God's talent scouts today
select for covenant without regard
for gender, reinterpreting His word
and that His holy detectives glossing the bush
(most likely wild acacia), His scholars of J
E and P deciphering Exodus
will fruitfully research the several ways
divine authentication lights up truth.
Fragments of it, cryptic, fugitive
still spark the synapses that let us live.

ANNE SEXTON

(1927–1974, American)

───

And One for My Dame

A born salesman,
my father made all his dough
by selling wool to Fieldcrest, Woolrich and Faribo.

A born talker,
he could sell one hundred wet-down bales
of that white stuff. He could clock the miles and sales

and make it pay.
At home each sentence he would utter
had first pleased the buyer who'd paid him off in butter.

Each word
had been tried over and over, at any rate,
on the man who was sold by the man who filled my plate.

My father hovered
over the Yorkshire pudding and the beef:
a peddler, a hawker, a merchant and an Indian chief.

Roosevelt! Willkie! and war!
How suddenly gauche I was
with my old-maid heart and my funny teenage applause.

Each night at home
my father was in love with maps
while the radio fought its battles with Nazis and Japs.

Except when he hid
in his bedroom on a three-day drunk,
he typed out complex itineraries, packed his trunk,

his matched luggage
and pocketed a confirmed reservation,
his heart already pushing over the red routes of the
        nation.

I sit at my desk
each night with no place to go,
opening the wrinkled maps of Milwaukee and Buffalo,

the whole U.S.,
its cemeteries, its arbitrary time zones,
through routes like small veins, capitals like small stones.

He died on the road,
his heart pushed from neck to back,
his white hanky signaling from the window of the
        Cadillac.

My husband,
as blue-eyed as a picture book, sells wool:
boxes of card waste, laps and rovings he can pull

to the thread
and say *Leicester, Rambouillet, Merino,*
a half-blood, it's greasy and thick, yellow as old snow.

And when you drive off, my darling,
Yes, sir! Yes, sir! It's one for my dame,
your sample cases branded with my father's name,

your itinerary open,
its tolls ticking and greedy,
its highways built up like new loves, raw and speedy.

DIANA O'HEHIR

(1929–   , American)

Summoned

Summoned by the frantic powers
Of total recall, sleeping pills, love;
Come down, come down, come down;
Wear red if you can, wear red
For suffering, jade for rebirth,
Diamonds in your front incisors,
A rope of orange stars—you were martyred, weren't you?
So wear a circle of gold thorns, prongs capped
In scarlet shell.

And bring with you, down, down, down,
A recollection of how you fell
Like Lucifer, morn to morn and night to night
For at least a year, your hair alight
Your rigid corpse a spoked wheel
Meteor trails ejecting from each thumb,
Sun eyes, a black light in your chest
Where the bare heart burned.

Oh, love, my love, my failure,
I can hardly bear, barely recall
The nights I ate ghosts, the nights
My shuttered, shivered window held
Three million savage stars and you;
Your spread arms splitting my sky, the light
Reflected in my own eye: your light, your might, your burn.

Come down. My sky-chart shows
Your cold corpse turning slowly, a black sun
Giving no light at all, reflecting none,
Aimlessly gentle, a twig on a pond
Circling. Gone, they say, gone, truly gone.
The eyes as blank as buttons, the mouth
Only an O. Never mind. Come down.
I can revive you. My passion is Judah, all artifice, all
     God.
I care with my breasts. I care with my belly's blood.
Come down.

ADRIENNE RICH

(1929–   , American)

———

(*Dedications*) from *An Atlas of a Difficult World*

I know you are reading this poem
late, before leaving your office
of the one intense yellow lamp-spot and the darkening
        window
in the lassitude of a building faded to quiet
long after rush-hour.   I know you are reading this poem
standing up in a bookstore far from the ocean
on a grey day of early spring, faint flakes driven
across the plains' enormous spaces around you.
I know you are reading this poem
in a room where too much has happened for you to bear
where the bedclothes lie in stagnant coils on the bed
and the open valise speaks of flight
but you cannot leave yet.   I know you are reading this
        poem
as the underground train loses momentum and before
        running up the stairs
toward a new kind of love
your life has never allowed.
I know you are reading this poem by the light
of the television screen where soundless images jerk and
        slide
while you wait for the newscast from the *intifada*.
I know you are reading this poem in a waiting-room
of eyes met and unmeeting, of identity with strangers.
I know you are reading this poem by fluorescent light

in the boredom and fatigue of the young who are counted
        out,
count themselves out, at too early an age.   I know
you are reading this poem through your failing sight, the
        thick
lens enlarging these letters beyond all meaning yet you
        read on
because even the alphabet is precious.
I know you are reading this poem as you pace beside the
        stove
warming milk, a crying child on your shoulder, a book in
        your hand
because life is short and you too are thirsty.
I know you are reading this poem which is not in your
        language
guessing at some words while others keep you reading
and I want to know which words they are.
I know you are reading this poem listening for something,
        torn between bitterness and hope
turning back once again to the task you cannot refuse.
I know you are reading this poem because there is nothing
        else left to read
there where you have landed, stripped as you are.

ELAINE FEINSTEIN

(1930–   , British)

―――――

England

Forgotten, shabby and long time abandoned
   in stubbled fur, with broken
teeth like toggles, the old gods are leaving.
   They will no longer crack the
tarmac of the language, open generous
   rivers, heal our scoured thoughts.
They will only blink, and move on, and
   tomorrow no one will remember their songs

unless they rise in warning, as when
   sudden planes speed overhead
crossing the sky with harsh accelerating
   screams. You may shiver then
to hear the music of the gods leaving.
   This generation
is waiting for the boy Octavius.
   They don't like losers.
And the gods are leaving us.

SYLVIA PLATH

(1932–1963, American)

———

Kindness

Kindness glides about my house.
Dame Kindness, she is so nice!
The blue and red jewels of her rings smoke
In the windows, the mirrors
Are filling with smiles.

What is so real as the cry of a child?
A rabbit's cry may be wilder
But it has no soul.
Sugar can cure everything, so Kindness says.
Sugar is a necessary fluid,

Its crystals a little poultice.
O kindness, kindness
Sweetly picking up pieces!
My Japanese silks, desperate butterflies,
May be pinned any minute, anesthetized.

And here you come, with a cup of tea
Wreathed in steam.
The blood jet is poetry,
There is no stopping it.
You hand me two children, two roses.

MARGE PIERCY

(1936–   , American)

———

Visiting a dead man on a summer day

In flat America, in Chicago,
Graceland cemetery on the German North Side.
Forty feet of Corinthian candle
celebrate Pullman embedded
lonely raisin in a cake of concrete.
The Potter Palmers float
in an island parthenon.
Barons of hogfat, railroads and wheat
are postmarked with angels and lambs.

But the Getty tomb: white, snow patterned
in a triangle of trees swims dappled with leaf shadow,
sketched light arch within arch
delicate as fingernail moons.

The green doors should not be locked.
Doors of fern and flower should not be shut.
Louis Sullivan, I sit on your grave.
It is not now good weather for prophets.
Sun eddies on the steelsmoke air like sinking honey.

On the inner green door of the Getty tomb
(a thighbone's throw from your stone)
a marvel of growing, blooming, thrusting into seed:
how all living wreathe and insinuate
in the circlet of repetition that never repeats:

[135]

ever new birth never rebirth.
Each tide pool microcosm spiraling from your hand.

Sullivan, you had another five years
when your society would give you work.
thirty years with want crackling in your hands.
Thirty after years with cities
flowering and turning grey in your beard.

All poets are unemployed nowadays.
My country marches in its sleep.
The past structures a heavy mausoleum
hiding its iron frame in masonry.
Men burn like grass
while armies grow.

Thirty years in the vast rumbling gut
of this society you stormed
to be used, screamed
no louder than any other breaking voice
The waste of a good man
bleeds the future that's come
in Chicago, in flat America,
where the poor still bleed from the teeth,
housed in sewers and filing cabinets,
where prophets may spit into the wind
till anger sleets their eyes shut,
where this house that dances the seasons
and the braid of all living
and the joy of a man making his new good thing
is strange, irrelevant as a meteor,
in Chicago, in flat America
in this year of our burning.

LUCILLE CLIFTON

(1936–   , American)

---

miss rosie

when i watch you
wrapped up like garbage
sitting, surrounded by the smell
of too old potato peels
or
when i watch you
in your old man's shoes
with the little toe cut out
sitting, waiting for your mind
like next week's grocery
i say
when i watch you
you wet brown bag of a woman
who used to be the best looking gal in georgia
used to be called the Georgia Rose
i stand up
through your destruction
i stand up

JUDITH EMLYN JOHNSON

(1936–   , American)

———

Sonnet: On Women's Business

the Great Emperor, like a snowflake, has laid his head
      on the line
we walk. i didn't know how not to kick him into the
      drifts.
don't be boring, the moths whispered, as they unraveled
      around the flame.
the snow will melt all of us soon enough, especially when
      these november drafts

teach us balance, the snow will flicker around you with
      greater blankness than mountains of kindness
      to snow can warm
or tides of consideration of moths can knit together. that
      small candle you stem will go white.
we shall go out / together / being boring. listen to that
      speaking head swarm
alive out of the snowdrifts. it wobbles. the bees have
      nested in its throat.

there is nothing you can do but make a fool of yourself,
      like a moth under the dead
sea tides. Magna Mater, this is not a popularity poll.
      there is no way you can reverse
the great snowjobs of policy. you are married to policy as
      to a coil of bees in a frozen head
that must sweep you in when they swarm. the tongue

flickers, the tongue thickens, that ball wavers,
     it cannot stay the course

but it wants you, listen to it hum how it wants you, it
          changes shape, it has risen to become a loaf of
          bread that chokes the deep
mold-ingrown snowbank gorge of history. you are married
          to history as to a heavy loaf /
                              there is no way it will keep.

MARGARET ATWOOD

(1939–   , Canadian)

———

from *Circe/Mud Poems*

It was not my fault, these animals
who once were lovers

it was not my fault, the snouts
and hooves, the tongues
thickening and rough, the mouths grown over
with teeth and fur

I did not add the shaggy
rugs, the tusked masks,
they happened

I did not say anything, I sat
and watched, they happened
because I did not say anything.

It was not my fault, these animals
who could no longer touch me
through the rinds of their hardening skins,
these animals dying
of thirst because they could not speak

these drying skeletons
that have crashed and litter the ground
under the cliffs, these
wrecked words.

I made no choice
I decided nothing

One day you simply appeared in your stupid boat,
your killer's hands, your disjointed body, jagged as a
        shipwreck,
skinny-ribbed, blue-eyed, scorched, thirsty, the usual,
pretending to be — what? a survivor?

Those who say they want nothing
want everything.
It was not this greed
that offended me, it was the lies.

Nevertheless I gave you
the food you demanded for the journey
you said you planned; but you planned no journey
and we both knew it.

You've forgotten that,
you made the right decision.
The trees bend in the wind, you eat, you rest,
you think of nothing,
your mind, you say,
is like your hands, vacant:

vacant is not innocent.

✿   ✿   ✿

There must be more for you to do
than permit yourself to be shoved
by the wind from coast

to coast to coast, boot on the boat prow
to hold the wooden body
under, soul in control

Ask at my temples
where the moon snakes, tongues of the dark
speak like bones unlocking, leaves falling
of a future you won't believe in

Ask who keeps the wind
Ask what is sacred

Don't you get tired of killing
those whose deaths have been predicted
and are therefore dead already?

Don't you get tired of wanting
to live forever?

Don't you get tired of saying Onward?

KELLY CHERRY

(1940–   , American)

Golgotha

And when they were come unto a place called Golgotha, that is to say, a place of a skull . . .
— MATTHEW 27:33

"Et uenerunt in locum qui dicitur Golgotha, quod est Caluariae locus." . . . Ex quo apparet Caluariae . . . locum significare decollatorum, ut ubi abundauit peccatum superabundet gratia ["And they came to a place called Golgotha, where Calvary is." . . . Therefore the name of Calvary appears . . . to signify "a place of the decapitated," so that where sin has abounded grace may be superabundant].
— JEROME, *Commentary on St. Matthew*

They were scattered on the hillside like stones,
polished by the wind-rag: the smooth, shining bones,
cheekbone and eye socket, the empty skull-cases

of brains that had vanished into various gullets, leaving
     no traces
of thought, not even a single, stray
idea. For much of that long, painful day

he must have contemplated the meanings of
erosion, mortal decay, vanity, impermanence, rather than
     love,
until in the lengthening light

that drew on toward – but he would never see it – that
      night,
he saw – a trick of his blood-blurred eyes, perhaps –
      them move,
and knew the meaning of the skulls was love

and knew the one proposition needing no proof
is that God exists because God thinks or is thought of.
God is what remains in the final analysis.

SHARON OLDS

(1942–   , American)

I Go Back to May 1937

I see them standing at the formal gates of their colleges,
I see my father strolling out
under the ochre sandstone arch, the
red tiles glinting like bent
plates of blood behind his head, I
see my mother with a few light books at her hip
standing at the pillar made of tiny bricks with the
wrought-iron gate still open behind her, its
sword-tips black in the May air,
they are about to graduate, they are about to get married,
they are kids, they are dumb, all they know is they are
innocent, they would never hurt anybody.
I want to go up to them and say Stop,
don't do it — she's the wrong woman,
he's the wrong man, you are going to do things
you cannot imagine you would ever do,
you are going to do bad things to children,
you are going to suffer in ways you never heard of,
you are going to want to die. I want to go
up to them there in the late May sunlight and say it,
her hungry pretty blank face turning to me,
her pitiful beautiful untouched body,
his arrogant handsome blind face turning to me,
his pitiful beautiful untouched body,
but I don't do it. I want to live. I
take them up like the male and female

paper dolls and bang them together
at the hips like chips of flint as if to
strike sparks from them, I say
Do what you are going to do, and I will tell about it.

LINDA GREGG

(1942–   , American)

———

Gnostics on Trial

Let us make the test. Say God wants you
to be unhappy. That there is no good.
That there are horrors in store for us
if we do manage to move toward Him.
Say you keep Art in its place, not too high.
And that everything, even eternity, is measurable.
Look at the photographs of the dead,
both natural (one by one) and unnatural
in masses. All tangled. You know about that.
And can put Beauty in its place. Not too high,
and passing. Make love our search for unhappiness,
which is His plan to help us.
Disregard that afternoon breeze from the Aegean
on a body almost asleep in the shuttered room.
Ignore melons, and talking with friends.
Try to keep from rejoicing. Try
to keep from happiness. Just try.

MARILYN HACKER

(1942–   , American)

———

Introductory Lines

Rushing to press, it still would seem evasion
not to compose a Verse for this Occasion
to introduce and celebrate our choices
of forms shaped by contemporary voices
(received forms, or invented, or adapted
from Norse, or Anglo-Saxon as one chap did).
At best form gives concinnity, precision,
paring of words and widening of vision,
play for the mind, focus that is self-critical.
Poets, and poems, are not apolitical.
Women and other radicals who choose
venerable vessels for subversive use
affirm what Sophomore Survey often fails
to note: God and Anonymous are not white males.
"We always crafted language just as they did.
We have the use, and we reclaim the credit."

One form perennially apposite,
the useful garment of the sonnet fit
lover, fabulist, feminist, and wit
—those categories not, of course, exclusive.
Concise, ornate, colloquial, allusive
language tidewashed Cathedral Station's floor,
low pun to philosophic metaphor.
A camera on a rotating boom,
six words spin slowly round and pan the room:

[148]

I would not like to have to choose between a
sestina on composing a sestina
and one that's a whodunit thirty-nine
lines long—and science fiction has a fine
champion, in sonnet sequence. Bible and fairy,
sexy, perverse, domestic, cautionary
tales are told, some controversy sowed.
There's one syllabic, one Pindaric ode.
There's birth, love, death, work, solitude (no money,
oddly enough). There's quite a lot that's funny,
and everything that's funny is not slight.
Poets who always, poets who seldom write
in forms, well-known or unknown, all responded.
(*Please* don't send whole verse novels, like someone did!)
A Wiccean muse, Form can transform like Circe.

P.S. There are no haiku; that's a mercy.

LOUISE GLÜCK

(1943–   , American)

———

The Triumph of Achilles

In the story of Patroclus
no one survives, not even Achilles
who was nearly a god.
Patroclus resembled him; they wore
the same armor.

Always in these friendships
one serves the other, one is less than the other:
the hierarchy
is always apparent, though the legends
cannot be trusted —
their source is the survivor,
the one who has been abandoned.

What were the Greek ships on fire
compared to this loss?

In his tent, Achilles
grieved with his whole being
and the gods saw

he was a man already dead, a victim
of the part that loved,
the part that was mortal.

SANDRA McPHERSON

(1943–   , American)

Eschatology

I accompany this life's events like a personal journalist:
"Little did she know when she got in the car that after-
        noon . . . ";
or "Despite inauspicious beginnings,
this was to be their happiest year."

Little did I expect that our horoscopes would prove true.
And how could we foresee an answer to
that frankly secular prayer, we with so little faith
as to be false prophets to our most fortunate gifts.

I am glad when doom fails. Inept apocalypse
is a specialty of the times: the suffering of the rich
at the hand of riches; the second and third comings of
        wars.

Shouldn't we refuse prediction
that the untried today is guilty, that immeasurable
as this child's hope is, it will break tomorrow?

TESS GALLAGHER

(1943–   , American)

———

Linoleum

for Mark Strand

There are the few we hear of
like Christ, who, with divine grace,
made goodness look easy, had
a following to draw near, gave up
the right things and saw to it
that sinners got listened to.
Sharpening my failures, I remember
the Jains, the gentle swoosh
of their brooms on a dirt path
trodden by children and goats, each
thoughtful step taken in peril of
an ant's life or a fat grub hidden
under a stick. In the car wash,
thinking of yogis under a tree
plucking hair by hair the head
of an initiate, I feel at least
elsewhere those able for holiness —
its signs and rigors — are at work.
Ignominiously, I am here, brushes
clamped, soap and water pulsing
against my car. (A good sign too,
those asylums for old and diseased
animals.) My car is clean

and no one has had to
lift a finger. The dead
bugs have been gushed away into a soup
of grit and foam — the evidence
not subterranean, but streaming along
the asphalt in sunlight so dazzling
I attend the birth-moment of
the word *Hosannah!*

I care about the bugs and not
in this life will I do enough towards
my own worth in the memory
of them. I appreciate the Jains,
their atonements for my neglect,
though I understand it makes poor farmers
of them, and good we all
don't aspire to such purity so
there's somebody heartless enough to
plow the spuds.

Early on, in admiration, I put off
knowledge, and so delayed reading about
the Jains — not to lose
solace. But in the county library,
turning a page, I meet them as
the wealthiest moneylenders
in Western India. Reading on,
I'm encouraged — the list of virtues
exceeds vices — just four
of those: anger, pride, illusion and
greed. The emphasis clearly on
striving. I write them down
in the corner of a map
of Idaho: forbearance, indulgence,
straightforwardness, purity,

veracity, restraint, freedom from
attachment to anything, poverty
and chastity.

Choosing, getting into the car to
get to the supermarket, hearing
over engine noise the bright agonies
of birds, the radio news with the child
nailed into a broom closet for
twenty-four hours by parents who
in straightforwardness sacrificed
forbearance, I feel a longing
for religion, for doctrine swift
as a broom to keep the path
clear. Later, alone in the kitchen
with the groceries, I read the list
again. Overwhelmed by the loneliness
of the saints, I take up my broom
and begin where I stand,
with linoleum.

EAVAN BOLAND

(1944–   , Irish)

———

The War Horse

This dry night, nothing unusual
About the clip, clop, casual

Iron of his shoes as he stamps death
Like a mint on the innocent coinage of earth.

I lift the window, watch the ambling feather
Of hock and fetlock, loosed from its daily tether

In the tinker camp on the Enniskerry Road,
Pass, his breath hissing, his snuffling head

Down. He is gone. No great harm is done.
Only a leaf of our laurel hedge is torn –

Of distant interest like a maimed limb,
Only a rose which now will never climb

The stone of our house, expendable, a mere
Line of defence against him, a volunteer

You might say, only a crocus its bulbous head
Blown from growth, one of the screamless dead.

But we, we are safe, our unformed fear
Of fierce commitment gone; why should we care

If a rose, a hedge, a crocus are uprooted
Like corpses, remote, crushed, mutilated?

He stumbles on like a rumour of war, huge,
Threatening; neighbours use the subterfuge

Of curtains; he stumbles down our short street
Thankfully passing us, I pause, wait.

Then to breathe relief lean on the sill
And for a second only my blood is still

With atavism. That rose he smashed frays
Ribboned across our hedge, recalling days

Of burned countryside, illicit braid:
A cause ruined before, a world betrayed.

CAROL MUSKE

(1945–   , American)

———

To the Muse

New Year's Eve, 1990

She danced topless, the light-eyed drunken girl
who got up on the bow of our pleasure boat
last summer in the pretty French Mediterranean.

Above us rose the great grey starboard flank
of an aircraft carrier. Sailors clustered
on the deck above, cheering, and the caps rained down,

a storm of insignia: S.S. *Eisenhower.*
I keep seeing the girl when I tell you
the *Eisenhower*'s now in the Gulf, as if

the two are linked: the bare-breasted dancer
and a war about to be fought. Caps fell
on the bow and she plucked one up, set it rakishly

on her red hair. In the introspective manner
of the very drunk, she tipped her face dreamily up,
wet her lips, an odalisque, her arms crossed akimbo

on the cap. Someone, a family member, threw a shirt
over her and she shrugged it off, laughing, palms
fluttering about her nipples. I tell you I barely knew

those people, but you, you liked the girl, you
liked the ship. You like to fuck, you told me.
The sex of politics is its intimate divisive plural,

we, us, ours, *Who's over there?* you ask — *not us.*
Your pal is there, a flier stationed on a carrier.
He drops the jet shrieking on the deck. Pitch dark:

he lowers the nose toward a floating strip of
lit ditto marks and descends. Like writing haiku —
the narrator is a landscape. A way of staying subjective

but humbling the perceiver: a pilot's view.
When you write to your friend I guess that
there are no margins, you want him to see

everything you see and so transparent is
your kind bravado: he sees that too. Maybe
he second-guesses your own desire to soar over

the sand ruins, sit yourself in the masked pit
and rise fifteen hundred screaming feet a minute
into an inaccessible shape: falcon, hawk — Issa's

blown petals? Reinvent war, then the woman's faithless
enslaved dance. Reinvent sailors bawling at the rail
and the hail of clichés: flash of legs on the slave deck.

Break the spell, reverse it: caps on the waves as they
toss away their uniforms, medals, stars. Then the girl
will wake up, face west, a lengthening powerful figurehead

swept gold with fire. The waves keep coming: the you, the
   me,
the wars. Here is the worst of it, stripped, humiliated –
or dancing on the high deck, bully-faced, insatiable.

Here is the lie that loves us as history personified,
here's the personification: muse, odalisque, soldier,
nightfall – swear to us, this time, you will make it right.

VERONICA FORREST-THOMSON

(1947–75, Scottish)

———

Strike

for Bonnie, my first horse

1

Hail to thee, blithe horse, bird thou never wert!
And, breaking into a canter, I set off on the long road
    south
Which was to take me to so many strange places,
That room in Cambridge, that room in Cambridge, that
    room in Cambridge,
That room in Cambridge, this room in Cambridge,
The top of a castle in Provence and an aeroplane in mid-
    Atlantic.
Strange people, that lover, that lover, that lover, that
    lover.
Eyes that last I saw in lecture-rooms
Or in the Reading Room of The British Museum reading,
    writing,
Reeling, writhing, and typing all night (it's cheaper than
    getting drunk),
Doing tour en diagonale in ballet class (that's cheaper than
    getting drunk too).
But first I should describe my mount. His strange colour;
He was lilac with deep purple points (he was really a
    siamese cat).
His strange toss and whinny which turned my stomach

And nearly threw me out of the saddle. His eyes
His eyes his eyes his eyes his eyes
Eyes that last I saw in lecture rooms
His eyes were hazel brown and deceptively disingenuous.
I got to know those eyes very well.
Our journey through England was not made easier by the
       fact
That he would eat only strawberries and cream (at any
       season).
And he wanted a lot of that.
Nevertheless I got here and the first time I ever set foot in
       the place
I knew it was my home. The trouble was to convince the
       authorities.
Jobs were scarce and someone with a purple-point
       siamese to keep
In strawberries and cream has a certain standard of living,
When I sold my rings and stopped buying clothes I knew
It was the end. When I cut down on food it was clear
I was on some sort of quest.
There was an I-have-been-here-before kind of feeling
       about it.
That hateful cripple with the twisted grin. But
Dauntless the slughorn to my ear I set.

2

How many miles to Babylon?
Threescore and ten.
Can I get there by candlelight?
Yes. But back again?
From perfect leaf there need not be
Petals or even rosemary.
One thing then burnt rests on the tree:
The woodspurge has a cup of three,

One for you, and one for me,
And one for the one we cannot see.

3

What there is now to celebrate:
The only art where failure is renowned.
A local loss
Across and off the platform-ticket found
For the one journey we can tolerate:
To withered fantasy
From stale reality. Father, I cannot tell a lie;
I haven't got the time.
Mirth cannot move a soul in agony.
Stainless steel sintered and disowned;
Stars in the brittle distance just on loan.
The timetables of our anxiety glitter, grow
One in the alone. The cosmic ozones know
Our lease is running out.
Deserted now the house of fiction stands
Exams within and driving tests without,
Shading the purpose from the promised lands
No milk our honey.
And the train we catch can't take us yet
To the blind corner where he waits
Between the milk and honey gates:
The god we have not met.

JANE KENYON

(1947–1995, American)

———

Let Evening Come

Let the light of late afternoon
shine through chinks in the barn, moving
up the bales as the sun moves down.

Let the cricket take up chafing
as a woman takes up her needles
and her yarn. Let evening come.

Let dew collect on the hoe abandoned
in long grass. Let the stars appear
and the moon disclose her silver horn.

Let the fox go back to its sandy den.
Let the wind die down. Let the shed
go black inside. Let evening come.

To the bottle in the ditch, to the scoop
in the oats, to air in the lung
let evening come.

Let it come as it will, and don't
be afraid. God does not leave us
comfortless, so let evening come.

CAROLYN FORCHÉ

(1950–   , American)

———

The Visitor

In Spanish he whispers there is no time left.
It is the sound of scythes arcing in wheat,
the ache of some field song in Salvador.
The wind along the prison, cautious
as Francisco's hands on the inside, touching
the walls as he walks, it is his wife's breath
slipping into his cell each night while he
imagines his hand to be hers. It is a small country.

There is nothing one man will not do to another.

MEDBH McGUCKIAN

(1950–   , Irish)

———

Teraphim

Deathly nameless angel, bend to my earth:
When you speak as fire should,
We become sweet water.
I wait for you like a road,
Without quite knowing that you wait,
My openness is like a name
Whose root you play on to say only
Something about yourself.

But only you can take me back
Beyond yourself, only you
Can change me by overhearing you speak.

When an earlierness,
Now forever forsaken,
Either way kisses us,
Like a natural radiance,
Or a story we were not born into,

Two paths we cannot distinguish between
Fold us into the lost
Strangeness of our namelessness,

The mist in which we are swallowed
Allows a garden to be planted,
To breathe with our breath.

Is it just this difference
That makes a difference,
Is it my name that you, more than a person,
Need or ask?

In the time a meaning ripens from your face,
An anxiety of touch and sight you cannot fill
Finds us in the garden we have felt before
That makes itself, where even the ground speaks.

BRENDA HILLMAN

(1951-   , American)

Mighty Forms

The earth had wanted us all to itself.
The mountains wanted us back for themselves.
The numbered valleys of serpentine wanted us;
that's why it happened as it did, the split
as if one slow gear turned beneath us . . .
Then the Tuesday shoppers paused in the street
and the tube that held the trout-colored train
and the cords of action from triangular buildings
and the terraced gardens that held camellias
shook and shook, each flower a single thought.

Mothers and children took cover under tables.
I called out to her who was my life.
From under the table – I hid under the table
that held the begonia with the fiery stem,
the stem that had been trying to root, that paused
in its effort – I called to the child who was my life.
And understood, in the endless instant,
before she answered, how Pharaoh's army, seeing
the ground break open, seeing the first fringed
horses fall into the gap, made their vows,
that each heart changes, faced with a single awe
and in that moment a promise is written out.

However we remember California later
the earth we loved will know the truth:
that it wanted us back for itself
with our mighty forms and our specific longings,
wanted them to be air and fire but they wouldn't;
the kestrel circled over a pine, which lasted,
the towhee who loved freedom, gathering seed
during the shaking lasted, the painting released
by the wall, the mark and hook we placed
on the wall, and the nail, and the memory
of driving the nail in, these also lasted —

JORIE GRAHAM

(1951–   , American)

In What Manner the Body Is United with the Soule

1

Finally I heard
    into music,
that is, heard past
    the surface tension
which is pleasure, which holds
    the self

afloat, miraculous
    waterstrider
with no other home.
    Not that I heard
very deep,
    but heard there was a depth,

a space through which
    you could fall,
an echo travel,
    and meaning
—small, jeweled, deep-water—
    flash. I heard

in a piano concerto
    the distance between the single instrument
and the whole

republic,
heard the argument each made
        for fate,

free will.
        And listened
to the piano, solo,
        on its gold hook, the tip
of the baton,
        struggle

and struggle.

2

From the mud
        of the Arno
in winter, 1967,
        we pulled up
manuscripts
        illuminated by monks

in tenth century
        monasteries.
Sometimes the gold letters loosened
        into the mud,
into our hands.
        We found

elaborate gold frames,
        Annunciations,
candlesticks. The ice
        the mud became
along the banks caught
        bits of sun

and gleamed.
    Eddies, twists, baroque knots
of currents,
    all the difficulties
of the passage
    of time

caught and held
    in the lush browns
we reached through
    blindly
for relics. It was
    almost spring,

we waded out further,
    the bells
in the churches
    kept up
their small
    warnings. The self, too,

is an act of
    rescue
where the flesh has risen,
    the spirit
loosened. . . .

3

Upstream the river
    is smaller,
almost still.
    On a warm day
the silence of the surface holds
    its jewels,

its tiny insect
        life.
In silence the waterstriders
        measure ripples
for meaning.
        They catch the bee

that has just touched
        the surface
accidentally. In silence
        the strider
and the backswimmer
        (its mirror image

underwater, each
        with ventral surface toward
the waterfilm)
        share the delicate
gold bee. They can both,
        easily,

be satisfied. They feed.
        Sun shines.
Of silence, mating striders make
        gold eggs
which they will only lay
        on feathers

dropped by passing birds
        or on the underside
of a bird's tail
        before it wakens and
flies off, blue and white and host
        to a freedom

it knows nothing of.

GJERTRUD SCHNACKENBERG

(1953–   , American)

———

Supernatural Love

My father at the dictionary-stand
Touches the page to fully understand
The lamplit answer, tilting in his hand

His slowly scanning magnifying lens,
A blurry, glistening circle he suspends
Above the word "Carnation." Then he bends

So near his eyes are magnified and blurred,
One finger on the miniature word,
As if he touched a single key and heard

A distant, plucked, infinitesimal string,
"The obligation due to every thing
That's smaller than the universe." I bring

My sewing needle close enough that I
Can watch my father through the needle's eye,
As through a lens ground for a butterfly

Who peers down flower-hallways toward a room
Shadowed and fathomed as this study's gloom
Where, as a scholar bends above a tomb

To read what's buried there, he bends to pore
Over the Latin blossom. I am four,
I spill my pins and needles on the floor

Trying to stitch "Beloved" X by X.
My dangerous, bright needle's point connects
Myself illiterate to this perfect text

I cannot read. My father puzzles why
It is my habit to identify
Carnations as "Christ's flowers," knowing I

Can give no explanation but "Because."
Word-roots blossom in speechless messages
The way the thread behind my sampler does

Where following each X I awkward move
My needle through the word whose root is love.
He reads, "A pink variety of Clove,

Carnatio, the Latin, meaning flesh."
As if the bud's essential oils brush
Christ's fragrance through the room, the iron-fresh

Odor carnations have floats up to me,
A drifted, secret, bitter ecstasy,
The stems squeak in my scissors, *Child, it's me,*

He turns the page to "Clove" and reads aloud:
"The clove, a spice, dried from a flower-bud."
Then twice, as if he hasn't understood,

He reads, "From French, for *clou,* meaning a nail."
He gazes, motionless. "Meaning a nail."
The incarnation blossoms, flesh and nail,

I twist my threads like stems into a knot
And smooth "Beloved," but my needle caught
Within the threads, *Thy blood so dearly bought,*

The needle strikes my finger to the bone.
I lift my hand, it is myself I've sewn,
The flesh laid bare, the threads of blood my own,

I lift my hand in startled agony
And call upon his name, "Daddy daddy" —
My father's hand touches the injury

As lightly as he touched the page before,
Where incarnation bloomed from roots that bore
The flowers I called Christ's when I was four.

THYLIAS MOSS

(1954–   , American)

Rush Hour

He boards the train downtown,
same time I get on in Lee Heights.

Eastbound passes westbound.
Can't pick him out,

square-shouldered every one of them,
under 40 years old, over 40 thousand a year,

never glancing up from their papers
till they pass Quincy, Central Avenue's

gutted brownstones, record and head shops,
Joe D's Tavern where I rent the back room.

He's ashamed of what we have in common.
I just left his house. Spotless.

COPYRIGHT ACKNOWLEDGMENTS

——

About the Editor

Carolyn Kizer has most recently edited *The Essential Clare* (1993) and *Proses: On Poems and Poets* (1994). She is the author of eight books of poetry, including *YIN*, which won the Pulitzer Prize in 1985 and an award from the National Academy and Institute of Arts and Letters; *The Nearness of You*, which won the Theodore Roethke Prize; *Mermaids in the Basement: Poems for Women*; *Carrying Over*, poems from the Chinese (ancient and modern), Urdu, Macedonian, Hebrew, and French-African; and *Harping On: Poems 1985–1995*.

Ms. Kizer was the founder and first editor of *Poetry Northwest*, a quarterly still flourishing after more than thirty years. She was the first director of literacy programs for the National Endowment for the Arts, resigning when then-president Nixon fired the chairman of the NEA, Roger Stevens. She has taught at various universities over the past twenty-five years, including Columbia, Princeton, and Stanford.

She is married to architectural historian and planner John Marshall Woodbridge and lives in Sonoma, California, and in Paris.